Dedicated to
Maureen
My beloved wife

SKIPPER'S YARNS

FROM

AVOCH

By

Donald Patience

ISBN: 978-1-905787-51-7

All profits will go to
For The Right Reasons Charity
Registered Charity no. SC037781

FOR THE RIGHT REASONS
MISSION STATEMENT

"To help people in Merkinch who have had the courage to free themselves from drug or alcohol addiction by helping them to stay clean and to aquire self-esteem, new skills and the confidence to apply those skills to sustain the profound changes they have achieved in their lives."

Published in 2010 by
For The Right Reasons
(Charity no.SC037781)
Printers, Publishers
38-40 Grant Street, Inverness
Tel 07717 457247
fortherightreasons@rocketmail.com

PREFACE

Sincere thanks are expressed to all those who assisted me in completing this short autobiography of my father's fishing life.

He retired due to ill health in his early 50's, taking up the role of grandfather, fishing & social activist, master builder of prawn creels and ferret and poaching nets for his pals in the Highlands.

All that knew my dad would despair at the current state of his beloved Fishing Industry and the treatment of the old, poor and weak in this proud Nation of Plenty.   (Donald Patience Sep 2010)

What's left for future generations?

CONTENTS

Childhood Days

For anyone in this shrinking world who has not heard of the village of Avoch, 'Auch', it is the largest, or was the largest, village on the Black Isle peninsula, possibly now overtaken by its neighbouring one of Fortrose. The Black Isle is virtually surrounded by water, on its northern side by the Cromarty Firth; its southern side is on the upper reaches of the Moray Firth which at Chanonry Point becomes the Inverness Firth up as far as the Kessock Bridge, where it then becomes the Beauly Firth and laps the south-western edge of the Isle. We then have the river Conon which flows into the Cromarty Firth on the north and the Beauly river on the south flowing into the Firth of the same name, leaving only a small piece of land between the two which is all that stops the Black Isle from being a true island. The name Black Isle has many origins, one being that it was once a massive forest but I tend to believe that it is because it enjoys one of the most temperate climates in Britain due to its being ninety-five per cent surrounded by the sea and sheltered by mountain ranges on the mainland, making it virtually snow free.

Having done my best to clarify the Black Isle, the village of 'Auch' is much more of an enigma. Situated between Fortrose and Munlochy on the north shore of the Inverness Firth, it could be considered to be one of the most cosmopolitan villages in Scotland. Whilst every village in the Black Isle had at one time a strong Gaelic influence, the language was never spoken in 'Auch', Avoch. They had a pidgin lingo of their own, one peculiarity of which being that many words ended in 'ie'. A young boy was a 'covie', a young girl a 'damekie' - a tap was a 'pumpie', 'skiff' being 'skiftie'; and many others. They also developed a manner of conversation of saying some words the opposite way round in a way that only they could understand - very often used when they were working beside Gaelic-speaking people at the gutting yards. I will not go into depth on this issue as it has died out now. Where our ancestors originated from is something that bamboozles historians, the present inhabitants having as they do the predominant names of Patience, Macleman, Skinner, Jack and Reid. The latter, according to our history teacher in Fortrose Academy, had moved north from the south of England, from somewhere around the London area. Miss Brown, our English teacher, was convinced that the Patience tribe were descendants of survivors of the Spanish Armada, a ship of which was wrecked on the Cromarty shore and from where they settled in Avoch. What gives credence to this theory is that when I was at school sixty years ago and the population of Avoch had about 600 Patiences, one outstanding fact was that only a few of them had fair hair and the majority could have blended in in either France or Spain. I was one of the throwbacks with blonde hair and my father once said of me "the biggest blunder I made in life was giving you Patience for a surname". My father was a strong influencing factor in my life - I would describe him as a gentleman of the highest order. He was a very humble, intelligent man, also a superb swimmer with a record of lifesaving, being awarded a silver watch at the age of 14 for saving John Alick White from drowning, and also gaining a further two certificates for other rescues (see back of the book for more info). I know of three more occasions, one being when he dived in to save a woman contemplating suicide off Stranraer pier, but the one which hurt the most, and where he came closest to losing his own life, was at the railway pier at Inverness where they were discharging the Kessock herring.

A boy was cycling down at the edge of the pier when suddenly one of his wheels went into the groove of the railway line and he catapulted into the swollen river. My father immediately leapt in and managed to grab hold of the boy but as he was wearing leather thigh-boots weighing

14lbs each they both went under. His brother Hugh threw out the lifebelt and, as my father said, he saw the glimmer of it as he was going under and with his free hand managed to grab it, thus saving both their lives. The fact that the boy's parents never thanked him for saving their son's life really hurt him. As did the fact that in those days the town of Inverness awarded £5 for the bravest deed of the year and this award was given to a local man who had merely waded out and pulled a girl to safety from between the two bridges.

Petty Officer Donald Patience - 1946

Another time, during the war when he was involved in minesweeping from Hartlepool as a petty officer, an air raid was in progress and there was an oil tanker on fire in the dock. He and two other men were sheltering between buildings beside the dock when a burning man appeared on the fo'c's'le of the tanker and tried to leap onto the dock. My father threw off his jacket and jumped into the water to save the seaman who shouted "save me but don't touch my hands". But he was forced to grab one of the man's hands as he was going under, and said later "I will never forget how the flesh was all melted away and it was only the bone that was left". All he found out was that the man was an Australian seaman, who died two days later in hospital, the same day as my father was drafted to Lowestoft to go for his skipper's ticket. He heard the following year that someone else had been awarded a medal for bravery for saving the unfortunate seaman, taking the credit for what *he* had done. As far as my father was concerned, however, the poor man would have died in agony so he was not interested in pursuing the matter. He said that in wartime you were only living from day to day - so that was it.

The pre-war days in Avoch, as in the rest of Britain, were described as the hard times, but a sense of humour helped and without a doubt we had a very compassionate society where sharing and helping your neighbour were part of everyone's life. Sadly this outlook has been replaced by a yearning to die the richest guy in the churchyard. One instance I can remember was in 1938 - the football coupon was done by most men in the village and my father won £36 for the number of draws, a fortune then. He gave each of the family £4 and I can still see the eight-day clock that adorned our mantelpiece which was my mother's gift from the winnings.

The village in those days was a hive of activity and small shops abounded. Two butchers, two shoemakers, two bakeries and about twelve other shops as well as two electricians, two tailors, a post office and a bank. But with the inevitable march of time, sadly all that character has now gone.

Avoch circa 1900

As the economy of Avoch was almost one hundred per cent dependent on the fluctuations of the elusive herring, the mothers had to purchase their essentials on 'tick', known locally as the 'blue book' where all debt was tallied up, hopefully to be settled up at the end of a successful fishing. Once when a woman went in to get more food and was told by the shopkeeper "I'm sorry, Maggie, you are owing far too much", she replied "oh well, I'll just take my custom somewhere else". But rather than lose a valued customer it was once again tagged on to the blue book.

To illustrate a few authentic anecdotes I will begin with the First World War ones. My mother's Uncle, Donald Jack, nicknamed 'Gaelic' (to avoid confusion between so many identical names most were given a nickname, me included) arrived at Whale Island in Portsmouth with a crowd of sailors from Avoch. An officer on the parade ground shouted to them "down here it's not only men we train, we train lions" and Donald Jack shouted in reply "back home we eat the bastards". Another rating, Tommy Yankee from Cromarty, when going through his medical was told "your teeth are in very poor condition, my man," to which he replied "they are good enough for all they are getting to do here, boy". Some older fishermen who were too old for active service were sent to Invergordon to work in conjunction with the naval fleet on lesser duties and were told on arrival that they would be billeted on board an old destroyer tied at the quay and were to live in No 14 mess. William, who was unacquainted with naval terms, commented "before I sleep in a mess I'll scrub her from stem to stern".

A meeting place in those days at Avoch was known as the 'lazy corner' - it was in the middle of the village and one day a travelling showman arrived with a dancing bear which performed for a time, witnessed by a large crowd. But when the exhausted bear had finished its performance and the owner went round with the hat, the crowd rapidly dispersed and when he addressed one woman and said "the bear can't dance for nothing", she replied "who bade him dance? - not me, anyway".

The fact that I grew up having the sea and its endlessly changing patterns on our doorstep was a deciding factor in my becoming a fisherman. During the winter months the Inverness Firth was one of the richest areas in Britain for herring, sprats and dolphins, amongst other species - a fact beyond dispute. A survey done by the White Fish Authority in the fifties proved that the Beauly Firth was the area richest in plankton in the British Isles. As every drift net fisherman experienced for himself, you got literally covered with them when shaking the Kessock herring from the nets. For such a semi-enclosed and shallow firth it is incredible that it was capable of supporting the immense shoals of herring and sprats which in the boom years of the sixties and seventies were being caught daily. At the peak of the boom some 200 boats were fishing there right round the clock. This was at the time when the method of fishing changed from the traditional drift nets to the ring net and pair and single trawl. When one realises that on many days well over a thousand tons of catch from this area alone were being landed at the various ports in the Moray Firth each day for a spell of four to five months at a time, these waters were then literally exploding with fish and the shoals must have been steadily replenished from the North Sea.

My earliest childhood recollection is of when I was six. One day in school I was violently sick and when I arrived home the doctor immediately rushed me away by ambulance to the Royal Infirmary in Inverness. It was peritonitis, in those days a life-threatening condition. That night in December is still engraved on my mind - there was a blizzard on and I had a raving thirst but in the ambulance they were only allowed to wet my lips with a damp handkerchief.

For the next few days everything was a bit hazy, but after a week my appetite increased and notwithstanding having drains in my side for over four weeks to clear up any infection, what sticks in my mind most was that the hospital mince was the best I had ever tasted. When after six weeks I was allowed home my mother had to listen to my whingeing incessantly telling her "you can't make mince like the hospital". But after that I made a complete recovery and from previously being a sickly child, I now had an insatiable appetite. Those were the days before antibiotics had been discovered and I owe my life to the surgeon and staff.

The following year World War II began and my father was called up into the Navy, first as a Petty Officer and then as skipper of various minesweepers, one of which was the trawler the *Merbreeze*, sweeping from Hartlepool.

Owing to the fact that his crew were mostly fishermen, he decided that one day a week they would trawl for fish for the other minesweepers and the base, and to compensate his crew for the extra work involved, make a nominal charge of one penny a pound for the fish which everyone considered to be a good deal. (One of the perks that we at home benefited from was that very often I would be told to go to our railway station at Avoch and collect a few stone of prime fish – turbot, plaice, to name a few - wrapped in wet sacking, which we shared out and thoroughly enjoyed).

Grandad, Skipper of Mine Sweeper
'Merbreeze' - Hartlepool 1946

The commander of the base, however, objected to this payment of one penny a pound for the fish. He stated "your navy pay is adequate". So the following week my father cancelled all fish to the base commander's office, and when the staff complained and my father told them the reason, saying "it's only fag money for the crew", the commander was basically 'sent to Coventry' by his staff. As they said, "forget the miserable sod, we want our share".

My memories are of a childhood very much influenced

by the sea, which in those days was alive with fish. During the winter months it was mainly herring and sprats; then came the summer period which abounded with flat fish - flukes, plaice, greybacks, dabs – and many other species including salmon, trout and lobster. The sea was so clean in those days that you could see the fish swimming about on the sea bed - the word pollution didn't yet exist. The burn which still flows through the village of Avoch also provided a wonderful pastime. I caught trout whilst wading and fishing with a 'hav', a cone-shaped net fastened to a circle of fence wire attached to a pole (similar to a landing net, for rod fishing). You pushed the hav under the overhanging bank and chased the trout into it by poking towards it with a stick.

The first few school years were really boring and my life only really began after school hours were over. I played all the usual childhood games, then as I got older my first major achievement came when the boat-building craze began. I was about ten or eleven years old and as we had a local saw mill at the station in Avoch, there was no shortage of wood, and no-one missed a few pieces 'borrowed' after dark. The old meal mill had a storage loft beside it and it was there that I obtained wood to provide me with the main planks for my boat. The store had a false floor of loose planks, about twelve feet long and a foot wide, ideal for my purpose. In those days the boats were all made like a punt with square front and back, but I had decided on a pointed stem, so I began by placing two planks together at one end, nailed a piece of 2" by 2" between then opened them out to a V wedge. Starting about four feet from the stem I then fitted pieces of plank across the boat approximately three feet apart and nailed the stern to another piece of 2" by 2" on each end of the planks. It was then I could see that boat building was where my future lay.

The local carpenter, undertaker Donald, was my next port of call, as he not only had nails but one of the most important components in boat building, tar. It was kept in a wooden barrel and for a few pence you could get a jugful. This was essential to have before the bottom could be nailed on. I started at the stem with the first piece of wood then spread tar between every piece and continued to the stern where the last piece projected about three inches. The seat was another piece of wood - nine inches from the bottom and three feet from the stern. By now I was totally absorbed in the building and tarring of this boat. My final brainwave was decking over the stem for three feet and then fixing on two three-inch strips in a V shape to spill any water back overboard. The proudest moment of my life was then 'The Launching', when I paddled into the sea and began my life as a fisherman. My father was in the Navy at the time which meant that my mother had sole responsibility for me and was kept fully occupied cleaning the tar off me and my clothes. That summer was one of the happiest in my life.

A lucrative pastime during wartime years was poaching rabbits. A friend, George Jack, and I started off with snares which we often found when roaming the countryside, obviously lost by the local trapper, Alex Logan, and any rabbits surplus to our needs found a ready market at 6d each. When my pal and I were able to purchase our first ferret we felt we had really moved into the big time and made ferret nets for ourselves. It was my first experience in net-making. On good days we could often end up with over two dozen rabbits, our only problem being the local trapper who in fact had the sole rights for catching them. After a few close shaves the inevitable happened. We were ferreting a large burrow at Balone Wood, with ten holes covered, listening out for the rumbling sounds of rabbits bolting, when the trapper, with his two dogs and gun, caught us red-handed. Nets, rabbits and most importantly the ferret which happened to surface at the wrong time, were all confiscated and a very sad team made its way home. However, after considering that I had nothing to lose, I decided to go to Bay

Farm and ask the trapper if I could have the ferret and nets back provided I promised that in the future our ferreting activities would be restricted to the railway bank as this was the only area not belonging to the Rosehaugh Estate. When I plucked up the courage to knock at the door the trapper's mother, Mrs Logan, appeared. She saw a dejected boy and after listening to my guarantees of curbing our future ferreting activities to the railway bank and, after a somewhat heated discussion with her son, I was handed back the ferret and nets but not the rabbits we had caught - and was assured in no uncertain terms that no more infringements of the law would be tolerated. This incident took most of the joy out of ferreting for us as at the age of ten the threat of a prison sentence hanging over our heads had a very profound effect. Every winter without fail the Kessock herring shoals would start arriving about September and last until the end of February. As my father was away at the war my brother and I helped ourselves to his herring nets. We would set one on the beach at low water and very often caught enough to supply all those who wanted some. We finally ruined his nets, but the thrill of going down in the early morning to face a shimmering silver blanket of herring made it all very worthwhile. During the time my father was skipper of a minesweeper he was at one stage out in West Africa where he picked up a twenty-six foot African dugout canoe which he brought back to the UK. As one of his skipper friends was returning to Scotland and passing through the Caledonian Canal he dropped it off at the sea lock in Inverness, from where we paddled it home to Avoch. Needless to say it was the talk of the village, but the twenty-six foot long canoe was too much for two boys to handle, so our father, on his first leave, cut ten feet off it and nailed on a flat stern. The hull was approximately three inches thick which resulted in its drooping at the stem.

Dugout canoe on the Okavango River, Botswana
donated by John and Janice Keist

This then required ballast to level it in the water, but I had to concede it was still superior to my first boat and as it required two to handle it we had to catch double the fish in order to make things viable.

A typical day's operation began at low tide digging for lugworm for our bait. I always dug from the eye to the shit which meant that when you sighted the head of the worm first, you could pull it out whole. On the stream tides when you had the big ebb - as the saying goes, "the guts of the ocean was dry" - a sandbank called the 'sanal sands' could be reached. This is where you got the best lugworm, so when you started digging for them the sandeels, six to eight inches long, would be spurting from the sand.

Fishing tackle consisted of six handlines, three a side, an old tin bath to hold the catch, a bottle of lemonade or milk and any kind of sandwiches. If mother was not in a good mood I would scrub out the stores. At that time we were still outside the EEC so I had no logbooks or flagships to trouble me - I was free to fish anywhere. Each handline consisted of a two-foot length of fence wire, with a loop in the middle and an eye at each end, and with a snood and hook weighted with a lump of lead in the centre. The anchor was scrap iron. As the boat was flat-bottomed I had an old tin for bailing out and also used an old towel. When I hit a good spot where the fish were biting fast, mostly with the flood tide, I could almost fill the bath from only a few spots. In about half an hour the run would be over, which meant I needed to up-anchor and shift to fresh grounds. On long summer days I would start in the morning and sometimes it would be the evening before the fishing trip was over.

Thankfully my mother realised that despite tar problems, irregular hours and ration books, I had to have a substantial meal waiting for me when I docked. This was consistent with Union rules. I realise now that my boat was a constant worry for my mother, especially once when I failed to return before dark and there was a strong southeasterly breeze blowing when the search party started out with torches. They walked by road to Munlochy Bay, then back along the shore and found the projecting three inches of plank which had snapped off the stern of my boat on the rocks outside Munlochy Bay. The problem had been that the boat had foundered and as the sea and wind had made it impossible to paddle back I had to tow it home. They had obviously thought that I had been lost but eventually found the bedraggled boy towing his vessel along the shore.

Shortly after this episode, on my way home from school, I saw a crowd on the beach watching a young boy, Roddy Matheson, about 8 years old, being blown out to sea on one of the punts that he must have pushed into the sea and boarded. By this time he was a few hundred yards out and obviously very frightened, and suddenly the punt capsized and he disappeared into the sea. A wailing sound erupted from the crowd but as my boat was there on the beach I paddled out to him, though by the time I arrived there all that was visible of him was the seat of his trousers keeping him afloat by an air pocket. I turned him face up and saw that his face was blue with foam around his mouth, but as my boat had only a few inches of freeboard it was impossible to drag him on board. All I was able to do was hang on to him and keep his head above water until a skiff with the harbourmaster and others arrived on the scene to resuscitate him and save his life. I paddled back to shore having completed my part in the rescue operation and was faced with my mother with a big axe. It was just the opportunity she had been waiting for for a very long time and she smashed up that pride of my life. Roddy's mother, Betty, who had five children, gave my mother a gift of half a pound of butter every second week for a long time afterwards, which with war time rations was very much appreciated. The following week I was presented at Avoch School with a brand new ten-shilling note for my part in the rescue. But my boat-building career was ended for ever.

I cannot remember any period of my life when I felt more at ease with the world than in those sunlit summers of my schooldays fishing in my own home-built boat. I was in perfect harmony with the ocean and for me no other way of life could give this freedom of choice. It didn't matter that at the end of each day my hands and bare feet were blanched from constant immersion in salt water and my fingers stained brown from baiting the lines with lugworms. All that was nothing compared with the satisfaction the day's catch gave me - there in the tin bath at my feet. Even half a century later the details and smells of the sea and the fish are as clear to me as when I experienced them.

When I began fishing at any chosen spot I dropped 'anchor', which was a lump of scrap metal. I then put down a line on each side (port and starboard) and held one in each hand. If no bites were felt during the next few minutes I would weigh anchor and shift grounds, as every line fisherman knows the thrill experienced when the fish strike immediately. Usually I would have the four baited handlines in operation, two on each side, for as long as the run lasted, which could be a few minutes or up to half an hour. I have to admit that a few times, what with the excitement of clearing tangled lines, unhooking fish, baiting hooks, it was a miracle that my boat didn't founder, although it did conform with all the basic DTI requirements.

One of my favourite fishing places had been at the mouth of Munlochy Bay, not because it was the best place, but because it was so peaceful and there was always an abundance of wildlife there. Seals basking on the beach, a constant coming and going of herons from the cove which is one of the few heronries in the North of Scotland, and plenty of other bird life as well - cormorants, seagulls and other wildfowl. Also, as I always felt that the cove had an air of mystery about it, that made it even more special for me. The fact that my boat was *capable* of going to Munlochy Bay said it all for a ten or eleven year old, as to me this was the equivalent of a deep-sea trawler going to the Arctic Circle. I was growing up then during the war when food was rationed, but because of the abundance of fish in those days (mostly plaice in summer and Kessock herring in the winter, caught on the shore with an old herring net), and being able to catch rabbits, I was kept active and ready and full of energy for any venture.

An incident that occurred when I was eleven years old and skylarking at Castleton Farm, where I leapt from a loft on to what I thought was a pile of straw below and damaged my knee cap on the cobblestone floor, was to cause me a major problem in later years. Some weeks afterwards, on the advice of our doctor, I went with my mother to the Royal Infirmary in Inverness to have it operated on, but no sooner had we entered the hospital than I turned chicken and was able to convince my mother that it was okay - so we made an about turn with me reckoning and hoping that it would rectify itself. Although being more than somewhat mistaken about this, it caused me very little problem in work, sport, swimming and various other activities until when in my late thirties it began to flare up and resultant x-rays showed it to be a matted mess, having been neglected for too long. The condition, osteo-myelitis, with a more-or-less constant seepage, is being controlled at present with antibiotics which seem to keep it stable. In the early eighties I began to suffer from osteo-arthritis which eventually resulted in my having both hips replaced in '88. This I was extremely fortunate to have had done as the knee infection had to be cleared up temporarily – otherwise, as the surgeon explained to me, there was every danger that it could contaminate the hip operations. The infection was controlled and with the skill of the surgeon and his team both operations were successful, otherwise I would have been wheelchair-bound for the past eleven years. The fact that I can never look good in a kilt is of no consequence as there is no such thing as a Patience tartan anyway. During the years preceding the hip replacements I was only able to continue fishing because of being skipper of the *Vision* and therefore not involved in manual work - mainly wheelhouse-bound and cooking the meals in the galley to break the monotony.

My schooldays up to the age of twelve in Avoch School provided me with the basics but I never had any enthusiasm for them. In fact at one time I hated school as another boy and I were both afflicted with a stammer and one particular teacher decided that the way to cure us was to start the day with both of us standing out in front of the class. My party-piece was to recite a list of words beginning with M, such as mother, monkey, money, which usually meant me humming like a badly-strung Stradivarius, whilst the repertoire of George Lee, the Minister's son, consisted of words beginning with B and produced a sound reminiscent of an angry hive. You can imagine the reaction of the rest of the class, and on reflection this treatment helped to create a rebellious streak in me as well as a distrust of authority. The following summer my uncle gave me the use of his fourteen-foot rowing boat, but as anyone who has built his own boat from DIY materials will understand, the thrill had gone. I then found myself in a very lacklustre period as I had to move to Fortrose Academy where my last two years were virtually wasted. The Black Isle was swarming with troops in preparation for the D-Day landings, and there were also three large tank landing craft tied up at the west side of the pier in Avoch. So I had very little interest in school and deliberately bungled my French exam and received only two marks out of one hundred. When presented with the corrected result covered with crosses I said to the furious teacher, who was built like an Amazon, "do I not get any marks for neatness?". This was the final straw for her and I received a well-deserved, resounding belt to my head that left me with a cauliflower ear for the next two days. When fifteen years old I decided to leave school and work with the Forestry - that lasted for nine months. Then I was offered the chance of a berth at the fishing as cook and I began my life as a fisherman. This was on my uncle's boat the *Boy Jim*, working the seine net in the Clyde. In those days this was the way that all fishermen started off at sea, but as cook I was a complete disaster. One day as we were heaving a bag of fish on board the bag started to burst - I dived over the side and held the split together. My uncle then put me on full wages rather than my having to spend the first year on half pay, which gave me a colossal boost.

Dugout canoe on the Okavango River

From the Clyde we arrived home to the Kessock fishing and the first pay packet was £36 per man, which compared with the forestry pay of £1.2s. was a small fortune. My father at this time decided that we would take a fishing boat on hire, the *Budding Rose*, and it was two years before we were able to build a boat of our own - the *Guiding Star*.

One episode I will never forget is the time when some Estonians were fleeing from Communism and on their way to the USA in two small white-painted boats about forty-five feet in length, the *Astrid* and the *Astervag*. They arrived in Stornoway where the townspeople supplied them with all they could give. Those small boats were packed like sardines with both old and young, and tied to the stringers were forty-gallon drums of fuel. The sight of them sailing into the Atlantic as the sun was setting, with their old chugging Bolinder engines, will always stick in my memory.

They arrived about fourteen days later in the States, safe and sound, where they were free to start a new life.

Both West and East Coasts in those days abounded with basking sharks and herring whales though it was mainly the Norwegian fishermen who pursued this type of fishing. They would harpoon one, and attached to the harpoon would be a length of rope with a massive float which would mark it, then if there were more about they would harpoon another. Only when they were dead would they take them on board when the float came to the surface. In 1947 we, along with the rest of the Avoch fleet, arrived home to the Kessock fishing where the shoals were abundant from Fort George to Nairn. There was also an excessive number of basking sharks, so many in fact that the fishermen requested the fishery cruisers to shoot them, which they did. This proved to be the most colossal blunder as afterwards the rotting carcases on the sea bed scared away the herring and ended the winter's fishing prematurely, proving once again that to interfere with nature is a dangerous policy.

The following year, 1948, our boat, the *Guiding Star*, was built by Walter Rickie of Anstruther, a boat which in those days I thought was an ocean-going vessel. It was fitted with an echo sounder, one of the first, and a 114hp Gardner engine. We decided in our ignorance to pursue the seine net, which Avoch fishermen were not then really adept at using, unlike the rest of the Moray Firth men, who were - Avoch fishermen were predominately ring and drift net. This was at the time when the control price was removed from all species of white fish, which ended up as a shambolic situation when the bottom totally dropped out of the market. I had been on board for three months and we had just started fishing in the Irish Sea when I was called up for National Service in the Navy.

National Service

My first impression of naval life in National Service, when arriving at Corsham, Wiltshire, and *Royal Arthur*, was of being just one of a mass of teenagers from all over Britain. First we were fed and watered, then came the medical inspection, where all our deficiencies were catalogued. I was told that my dentures were buck-teeth and would be replaced at His Majesty's expense to further enhance my good looks. We were then allocated our living quarters - large Nissen huts - and as the camp was divided into four areas, each sector containing around 1000 men, some order became established.

The following day, before being kitted, out we had to attend the barber's shop (a lady named Phoebe) to have a naval-style haircut - cost, 6d. This was at a time (1948) when luxuriant heads of hair were considered to be the height of fashion, and it would have been a waste of time and naval caps if your head were several sizes smaller after the haircut. Along with some 15 others, I was taken to Phoebe's establishment where we sat on benches around the wall to await our turn. Long hair for a fisherman would have been an inconvenience so I personally had nothing to worry about. In fact I was thoroughly enjoying the 'performance' - watching Phoebe, centre stage, inserting the electric clippers at the back of someone's head, seeing the clippers vanish, then emerge again from the clumps of hair dropping down onto the floor - this being accompanied by moans and groans from most of the spectators - one or two were actually in tears. Phoebe, keeping a sphinx-like expression on her face whilst wading through the discarded locks, would indicate to the Petty Officer in attendance to send across whoever was next in turn. To me it was one of the funniest experiences so far. Nevertheless I had the savvy to realise that to laugh outright would be inviting trouble with some of my National Service companions as losing their crowning glory was obviously a traumatic experience. Next day we were kitted out with our Navy clothes - bell bottoms, etc. - but after my trying on the tops and bottoms in stock it turned out that I was one of the very few whom nothing would fit. So I was measured for a complete rig-out and told that this would take six weeks; until it arrived I would have to wear my civvy clothes, and I was given the job of block cleaner along with my normal training.

The dining hall in the camp held tables which seated eight, and one person collected eight portions at a time for his particular table with a frame that could hold eight plates. I had been accustomed to a seaman's double rations, one of the perks given to the fishing industry, and now came up against a diet which was totally inadequate for my fisherman's constitution. But this did not pose a problem for long as most of my friends there were fishermen and it was our common practice to consume the first helping, place the empty plates under the table and go back for second portions, which had to be served in quantities of eight. Our system worked really well until one day I was placed at a table with a group with more 'refined' appetites. As I was the first to finish, I grabbed the tray, went up to the serving area for second helpings and arrived back at the table to find that the others were still slowly consuming the first helping. I told them to scoff it quickly as the Petty Officer in charge of the dining room was fast approaching. One of them turned to me and said, "We don't want any more, you gannet" by which the time the Petty Officer had arrived at our table and I was still left with four helpings on the tray. He immediately realised what was going on and took me to the Commander's office post-haste. Finally he could now explain why the kitchen was running short of rations every day. On our arrival at the CO's office the Petty Officer was asked to leave after had he explained that I had consumed five main courses and the CO asked why I ate so much. I told him that I had been accustomed to a seaman's rations and was still going through a transitional period, but that it would not happen again. He then asked if I was in any way connected with a Donald Patience who had been skipper of a minesweeper, the *Merbreeze*, based at Hartlepool, as he himself was also an ex-minesweeper skipper and a pal of his. On hearing we were related he told me to give my father his best regards and at the same time told me to be more careful in future. Meanwhile the Petty Officer had been patiently waiting outside the office and had fully expected I would begin a punishment immediately, so it came as somewhat of a surprise to him when I told him that the Commander had fully understood my dilemma and had let me off with a warning.

Donald & Jeff Peterson - Trafalgar Square, London

His response was, and I quote, "Good God, what's the Navy coming to?"

In the canteen for tea and a cake for which we had to queue up, very often if you were at the end of the queue, you could miss being served. For such as I, used to double rations and having, I must admit, a voracious appetite, this assumed a great importance. One day I had to go to the Commander's office with a request form, and on my arrival he was busy on the phone and I picked up a blank O.H.M.S. form from a pile on his desk. Back at the block I wrote on it "this is to certify that Ordinary Seaman Donald Patience, owing to the nature of his special duties, has my permission to go to the front of any queue. Signed, Commander Brown".

I enjoyed this concession for about two weeks, until one day a heated argument began with a chap whom I had attempted to precede with my form. Right out of the blue a Petty Officer appeared, took me aside and grabbed the form from my hand, saying "what in the so-and-so is this? I've been fifteen years in the Andrew Navy - do you know what you are looking at here, Jock? 90 days over the wall for forgery!". To my good fortune he was an Aberdonian, also an ex-fisherman with a sense of humour. "If you reckon being a block sweeper is special duties, the sooner you are back gutting fish for your health's sake, the better. But from now on keep your nose clean". This was a warning that I never forgot - forgery was out, full stop.

What became obvious in those first few days at *Royal Arthur* was that people from similar backgrounds and areas quickly merged into groups; Cockneys, Scousers, Glaswegians, Geordies, etc - whilst fishermen from all over Britain had a common bond, evident from their bigger-than-average hands, and even at that tender age were a breed apart. The differences in culture blended in as time went on and later I made friends from all walks of life, although predominantly from the fishing sector.

My biggest problem was in accepting discipline, which was also apparent in a few others, but in my case this rebellious streak continued throughout the whole of my National Service time, all too often to my detriment, as I had frequent spells of 'No 8's' (punishment for minor infringements of the rules).

My status as block sweeper, plus my having to wear my civvy suit (now somewhat the worse for wear) whilst everyone else in the block was kitted out in naval rig, did nothing for my self esteem. One morning when I had swept all the rubbish into a neat pile a tall Cockney, one of a group and one who considered himself something of a comedian, slid off his bed and kicked the pile of rubbish all over the floor, saying "right, haggis, you'll have to start again, but this time do it properly". I grabbed him by the throat - the bed capsized under him, scoring his back in the process - and he screamed "the mad bastard's broken my back, get him off me". The fact that he was able to sweep up the mess he had made proved that no permanent damage was done to his spine, and for the rest of the time in the block we were on a friendly basis.

What I very soon realised was that despite that common bond all fishermen had, the lifestyle of the deepwater trawlermen from Hull, Grimsby, Fleetwood, etc. was infinitely harder than that of our type of fishing. A trawlerman's life consisted of at least three weeks at sea, all too often in the most dangerous waters in the world, and on landing just 48 hours at home before setting out again. What did surprise me was that beneath their tough exteriors they all shared a love for the top classical singers - Caruso, Gigli, and the rest - and were generous to a fault but had a deep disregard for 'flannel', which at that time the Navy thrived on. The smallest rating in our group was Jeff Peterson, a trawlerman from Cleethorpes at Grimsby, a friend of mine I shall never forget. I found out a few years ago that he was lost at sea on his first trip as skipper of one of a pair trawler team heading for northern waters. He disappeared when coming from the fo'c's'le to the wheelhouse. It was thought that possibly the sharp motion of the small vessel compared to that of the big trawler to which he was accustomed could have cost him his life. He was determined from the beginning that National Service was a waste of time for him, and during the third week at *Royal Arthur* when we were undergoing a lecture from an elderly Petty Officer concerning the dangers of unprotected sex, he shouted "why waste our time, you've never had it". After the laughter subsided the PO said "whether I've had it or not, I'm wasting my time with you lot. Class dismissed".

When we were later transferred to Chatham, one pay-day Jeff had it calculated that he was now due his full pày of £2.10s. as he had completed his stoppage-of-pay period, and he, Bob Pennock and I were looking forward to a night ashore for a few pints. We were paid in alphabetical order - off caps, paybook placed on top - and Bob Pennock and I were both paid the full whack, but when it was Jeff's turn the Paymaster Commander said "Peterson, shillings ten". Jeff's face turned brick red but he calmly screwed the ten bob note into a ball and hit the Commander in the face with it, saying "keep it, you need it more than me", resulting in more punishment. His next scheme was trying to prove he was mentally unstable, which, if proved, would result in instant demob. He underwent a few sessions with the Medical Officer and on one occasion began stacking everything on the MO's desk in a neat pile. The PO who was present tried to stop him, but the MO said "no, leave him, I am studying his reactions". When Jeff had piled up everything available he placed the ink bottle on top and chucked the lot onto the MO. But it was all to no avail and Jeff, Bob and I were later drafted to the *Cleopatra* with every intention of becoming model sailors. As previously mentioned, because of my size I could not be rigged out with an off-the-peg uniform and had to wait six weeks until a made-to-measure one was ready. It was common practice to be allocated the job of block sweeper until you were rigged out properly, but after four weeks I decided to wash my suit. The result was so much shrinkage that the padding on the shoulders came adrift and did absolutely nothing to enhance my appearance. However a much bigger problem arose. There was a spate of thefts in the block, all kinds of articles going missing from the lockers, and everyone was investing in combination locks, including me. For large periods of the day I was the only occupant of the block and through boredom I started fiddling around with my combination lock to see if I could figure out the code.

Donald with his made-to-measure
Navy suit with 37 inch bellbottoms

The lock was made with four round discs and on turning the end disc I could detect a slight easing when it was in the right position, so I went on to the next and got the same result, which meant that once you understood how they were made they became totally worthless. With hindsight, to say that I was naïve over this is putting it mildly, - when everyone returned to the block, some with their newly purchased combination locks which were either numeric or alphabetical, they felt that their lockers were now safe from any thief - until I stupidly boasted that I'd bet two bob that I could open any one within five minutes. I had not realised that as block sweeper I was the prime suspect. After successfully opening three in succession the atmosphere was becoming increasingly hostile towards me but it was only when someone asked me what my occupation was 'outside' and I replied "a fisherman" and he then said "Yes, we know what you were fishing for", that the penny finally dropped. It was only the fact that my friends were trawler men that saved me. Thankfully, just two days later we had a crash inspection search of all the lockers, the result of which was that the two thieves were caught and my spell in Coventry ended.

For the first month of training we were confined to camp and given just one day shore leave, as it was termed, when most of us made for the nearest town of Bath. My father, as mentioned earlier, had been a skipper of minesweepers during the war and was also a heavy smoker. I could remember times, when I was still a youngster, when the odd parcel of Navy shag 'rolling tobacco' arrived at our house, and during that first month of training I managed to procure three tins of this which I sewed up in two handkerchiefs bought from the Navy stores for 6d each and inserted in my crotch area. This was in mid-summer temperatures which were in the eighties. The first obstacle getting past the sentries at the gate undetected, which I did with a slightly pregnant appearance, was overcome quite easily, but by the time I got to Bath it was a rather sodden bundle I had to wrap up in parcel paper to post home, as I had been sweating heavily all through my mission. My mother had a hatred of smoking and I never found out if the contraband ever arrived at its destination. It's possible that when she opened the package she dumped it in disgust and my efforts at smuggling were wasted.

Our next transfer was to Chatham barracks where we encountered the full weight of naval authority and square-bashing was the order of the day. Our honeymoon period was over, full stop - the odd misfit had been weeded out at Corsham. One happened to be a friend of mine who had been brought up in a secluded world where he had been accustomed to having his own valet and was totally unable to fit into the real world of dhobying your own washing. My next brush with authority was in the dining hall at Hawke block. I was going up for a second helping of soup from the large family aluminium urn at the table when the officer in charge of the dining room said "we have an Oliver Twist in our midst". He asked me why I did not ask if anyone else wanted more as there were about sixty ratings at the table. I remained dumb and could only look at him and think that he must have got out on the wrong side of the bed that morning. But because of my continued silence, and as we were now the focus of everyone's attention, the incident resulted in ten days' stoppage of leave for me for silent contempt - this was my first punishment in the Navy. It was at this time that it became obvious to me that to satisfy my above-average appetite I would have to be more devious in procuring the extra food needed for square-bashing and all the other activities we were involved in.

After about a month at Chatham we had been instructed in most of the basics of naval training. First came discipline, then gun drill, followed by depth charges, torpedoes, and also the most lethal of all, germ warfare. It was then that I found out that anyone interested, and having passed basic exams, could enter for a Sub-lieutenant's course at Plymouth. This was exactly what would make my term in the navy worthwhile as our fishing boat required the skipper to have a 'ticket' as it was over twenty-five tons. The course was due to commence in a fortnight's time and we were told what books were required - which then cost about £6 and the money for which I phoned home. We had to go to some offices before starting the course, and on the day I arrived at the classroom with all the other participants. The officer started by asking everyone his name and how long he had signed on for, which varied from five to ten years. When I said in my turn that I had enlisted for National Service he told me the course "was not for the likes of you" and asked why I had enrolled. I explained that if I passed the course it would be equivalent to the 'ticket' I needed for the Guiding Star after demob, to which he replied "Do you expect Her Majesty's Navy to squander money on you and allow you to enroll on this course for your own benefit when you go back to the fishing?" My reply was that it would make more sense than scrubbing paintwork and doing other menial duties. He then said it was a requirement to have had six months' sea time so I told him that I had already had three years'. He explained that it had to be Naval sea time and that the course was only for regular Navy personnel - which had not been mentioned previously. Some time later I met a fellow National Serviceman in Gibraltar who had been called up at the same time as me and was now a Sub-lieutenant. I asked him if he had signed on full time - he had not. I realised then that the class system operated in Her Majesty's Navy too. His father was a Lord.

****

National Service Sea Time

My next draft was on the *Cleopatra*. She was a light cruiser and it was the highlight of my time in the National Service.

Light cruiser Cleopatra

We set off for a cruise and combined operations with the French and Dutch navies and I had the thrill of experiencing the *Cleo* at maximum speed of about thirty knots. One of my duties was bowman on the Captain's barge, a high speed boat, and while at anchor in Douarney Bay we set off to collect the French Admiral from the aircraft carrier, *George Leuges*. It was as we were taking him to our ship that once again I blotted my copybook. There was a heavy swell lifting us up and down the gangway which was set in three stages and this meant a constant shifting of my boathook. The Admiral had to retreat a few times as the swell rose and fell before stepping on board, and unfortunately at the critical time of his final step, the boathook was pulled out of my hands, our bow swung out, and the Admiral ended up in the drink. He was recovered in record time but in a very bedraggled condition. A French officer dived in and salvaged his headgear. Because I have a tendency to see the funny side of things, but as usual had picked the wrong moment and had burst out laughing, it cost me fourteen days 'number elevens' on a charge of disgracing Her Majesty's Navy.

A constant source of irritation, when as bowman on the barge, was being continuously sprayed with water whilst standing in the cockpit, as it meant that the blanco on my cap dripped endlessly onto my blue top. One of my pals, Bob Pennock, who was in charge of the paint locker in the *Cleopatra,* and I had a brainwave regarding the solving of this problem for my cap. A coat of white flat paint, then gloss white and no more messy blanco. It went well until the following weekend in Gibraltar when the ship's company had fallen in on the quarterdeck for the Admiral's inspection with our Captain and the ex-Captain of the *Cleo*, Admiral Sir Philip Vian. They stopped behind me, scrutinised my immaculate cap and then lifted it off. I was asked in no uncertain terms what I had done to it. I explained that I could not see the sense of using blanco when a couple of coats of paint solved the problem, but this fell on deaf ears, my cap was unceremoniously chucked into Gib. harbour and I was told that any further attempts to revolutionise Her Majesty's Navy would land me in very serious trouble. Had I settled for one coat of flat white paint possibly the blanco would have been obsolete, but the addition of high gloss was a bridge too far. Because I was let off with a reprimand I considered myself to be very lucky and from then on toed the line on the blanco issue!

Another small incident occurred when I was on gangway watch on board the *Cleopatra* checking all crew members as they were coming on board. When our Captain, on boarding, told me that I had failed in my duties, I said "I saluted you, Sir", to which he replied "yes, but you didn't ask me to produce my passport". I had said "it's OK, carry on, I ken you". Apparently this became a standing gag in the wardroom, but, as the Captain understood, a National Service fisherman would have to be given time to conform to Naval protocol.

Cleopatra in Cagliari, Sardinia

Our next port of call was Cagliari in Sardinia and it was there, whilst on shore leave with my shipmates, that we all decided to indulge in some local wine, me for the first time in my life. After arriving on the last liberty boat back to the *Cleo* we fell into line on the quarterdeck to be inspected by the officer of the watch. His attempt at getting us to stand to attention was in vain as by that time we were all past the breathalyser stage, but it triggered my weak spot and I went into an uncontrollable fit of laughter, only to be joined by the rest of my mates. The officer's reaction was "rightho,

Commander's report in the morning". That following morning we were all in a very subdued state when we lined up on the quarterdeck. The Commander was at his desk and just as I was going up to it my pal whispered in my ear "that cod-eyed sod is going to swoon". As I marched towards him I could not help concentrating on his protruding eyes, and that set me off again and I burst out laughing once more. The response to this outburst was "I'll wipe the smile off that silly so and so's face, fourteen days 'number elevens', the rest - dismissed". This was diplomacy at its best, everyone joined in the laughter, even the Commander, and I was the only solemn one leaving the quarterdeck!

After Cagliari our port of call was Leghorn in northern Italy. It was still badly damaged from the effects of the bombardment and shelling from the British Navy and the atmosphere was still very anti-British, but this did not prevent us from trading with the bum-boats - open skiffs, laden with local handicrafts such as plaster ornaments of the Leaning Tower of Pisa and other tourist paraphernalia. This practice was classed as illegal by the Navy as it involved duty free cigarettes, tobacco and clothing amongst other things, but I was able to get a pair of parrot bookends for an old pair of Navy jeans. This trading was soon over (conducted through the portholes) as without warning the high pressure hose on the foredeck was turned on and blasted at the occupants of the two skiffs, reducing all their wares to rubble. Personally I thought this was pathetic and would only foster more anti-British feelings. We were docked there for a few days and I had one run ashore with my pal Jeff, when we travelled to Pisa and were photographed beside the Leaning Tower, but as the general feeling seemed to be definitely anti-British we were only too glad to sail away. We had encountered a similar situation earlier in our cruise. This was when we were involved in the combined operation with the French and Dutch fleets and had a few days in Brest, which was also still suffering the effects of a naval bombardment and feeling was running high with ill-will towards the British. This I can vouch for as my right thumb-joint was damaged in a fight with a crowd of French sailors whom I and two friends encountered after getting lost in the town. I had innocently approached them to ask for directions back to the docks in my own version of French, which, with the effects of the vino we had partaken of, was not quite up to their standard! I think we were only saved from total annihilation by the arrival of a patrol wagon into which we were all bundled and delivered back to the docks - still thankfully in one piece.

I always took any opportunity of improving my financial status, one of which was when I was made 'captain of the heads' and washroom cleaner, together with a pal of mine. We began a dhobi (washing) business; washing hammocks at one shilling a time, bed covers for 6d. For our 'business' we procured a five-gallon drum of tepol, which was used for bleaching the decks, and our programme was to first bung up the drain plughole in the wash place, then turn on all the showers and taps, flood the area to the depth of about a foot and pour out about two and a half litres of tepol. After this we had to wade through back and forth a few times, drain, then fill up with clean water and eventually let the area dry off. Our scam unfortunately had to go into voluntary liquidation due to the lack of space in the drying room and after a small problem that arose after we had hung up a few of the hammocks between the funnels during the night - they had blown away in a gale.

Another port of call was Casablanca in West Africa. We had moored up alongside a causeway which enabled us to dump off the slops from all the mess decks on the sea side of the causeway. It was the first time in my life that I saw real poverty. To see human beings rake through the garbage and salvage any scraps just to enable them to survive makes me realise, even now, half a century later, that little has changed in many parts of the world. It only emphasises strongly how little we have progressed between then and now.

We were there for a week and on my first day ashore I went aboard a fishing boat, being naturally interested in fishing. Very soon I got involved with the crew and that was

Local fishing boat - Casablanca

when one of my tins of ticklers (tobacco) which I had smuggled ashore was enjoyed by all the crew. We conversed in a mixture of pidgin English and our local dialect, broad 'Auchie'. I asked the skipper if I could go out for a trip with them as they were sailing the following day, and as by this time I had demonstrated that I could also repair the net. Their only request was that I brought some more tobacco, and then I would be one of the crew. On arrival back at the *Cleo*, my request was turned down by the divisional officer as he said "Patience, this is the Royal Navy, not a joyride for bored fishermen". On my next run ashore I was asked by some of the older seamen in the mess if I could smuggle a couple of bottles of brandy back as they could not be bothered going ashore. My method of doing this was to slip the bottles into my long naval socks which I then tied at the top with a handkerchief, and as we wore thirty-six-inch bell-bottom trousers they hid the contraband beneath them and my mission was duly accomplished. I arrived back with two bottles of four star Martell at two shillings & sixpence each as shown on the label. Once aboard they told me it was palm brew(!) and in no way fit for their consumption but I decided to prove a point and consumed a few mugs of it myself. My next recollection was waking up the following morning lashed to my hammock and to be faced with a trail of destruction - apparently I had gone berserk. Yet another lesson learned. We had met a similar situation earlier on in our cruise, which I mentioned earlier, when ashore in Brest.

We sailed from Casablanca the following Sunday and I had to go to the bridge with mugs of kye (tea) for the officer of the watch. It was there that I could observe what was showing on the echo sounder. It was the same type as we had on our own fishing vessel at home, a Kelvin Hughes admiralty type, and was showing a massive shoal of fish, possibly pilchards or sardines. The officer told me that we had been steaming through the shoal at twenty-five knots for the best part of two hours without its once losing the density. This was proof enough for me that this was what was going to revolutionise the fishing industry. With its ability to locate shoals of fish, show density and ground discrimination, my future was without doubt back to fishing and as soon as possible.

We arrived back at Chatham docks at the end of our cruise, which was after the Yangtse incident in which both the destroyer the *Amethyst* and heavy cruiser the *London* had been involved. I was with a squad which was detailed to remove all furnishings from the *London* as it was going to the breakers' yard. I was in the Captain's cabin, which we had been told to clear out, when I saw a few of his caps with the badges intact. I quickly cut these badges off as a souvenir rather than, as I thought, let them be just dumped.

However, a few minutes later over the tannoy system we were all ordered to fall in on the quarterdeck, immediately. On the way aft I asked one of the killicks what the panic was. He said some crazy sod had cut off the badges from the Captain's caps - but fortunately I was passing the heads, so at the time of the search they found no evidence!

I was next transferred to the *Soberton*, which was one of a tier of three destroyers moored in the Medway with skeleton crews on board. It was one of our duties to keep watch on these tiers of destroyers which were all moored to buoys up the Medway in a cocooned state of readiness. I was bowman on the liberty boat from the *Soberton* to the shore. I was becoming increasingly bored with the routine as it was all an anti-climax to my life on the *Cleopatra*, and one particular day after I had been charged with playing cards during working hours, I was sitting in the covered-in engine compartment of the liberty boat waiting to take the off-duty watch to the shore. I was smoking a 'tickler' when the killick came on board, spotted me smoking and reported me for smoking on a petrol launch - yet another charge. They say that things happen in threes. That night I had the dead watch on the tier of destroyers ahead of ours, between twelve and four am, and was up on deck at two am when I heard the sound of an engine, which I thought was a plane. Shortly afterwards I settled down in the Lower Steering Position where there was a small electric fire and dozed off, only to be awakened by the sound of boots on the steel deck overhead and then to be confronted with a PO and two ratings and charged with being suspectedly sleeping during watch. Luckily I happened to be outside the LSP on that encounter. The PO said they had hailed the ship at one forty-five am with no response, boarded and had been searching for the watch-keeper until two-fifteen, believing him to be asleep. The following day two of my friends, down for their annual fortnight's training in the R.N.R., arrived on board to invite me to go ashore with them. I had been confined to ship and was waiting on the Captain's verdict, not expected until the next day, and wondering on the outcome of my triple charges, so I could not go with them. I consulted some of the regular seamen on what I could expect as punishment and they unanimously agreed that I should prepare for at least ninety days 'over the wall', which is the naval term for imprisonment. They elaborated on this and told me that in wartime it could carry the death penalty. This particularly applied to the sleeping-on-watch incident. It was a regular procedure for the guard boat to steam up through the tide, stop the engine and drift down with the tide to try to catch an unwary watchkeeper not on watch on deck, and charge him.

I suddenly remembered that my pal, Bob Pennock, had the identical watch on the *Soberton* and I asked him what time the guard boat had hailed him. He checked in his log book and told me that it had been at two-o-five that morning, and as they were on the tide side of my tier it would have been at least five minutes later when the boat arrived at the tier of destroyers I was watchkeeping on. The following day when being charged by the PO of the guard boat, who stated that after hailing at one forty-five and getting no response, he boarded and eventually confronted me at two-fifteen, I said that at two am I had been on deck and had heard a sound which I had taken to be a plane, then, as I thought I had smelt something burning, I had gone below to investigate the lower decks. I told them that I had found an electric heater on and that it was on my leaving the Lower Steering Position that I was charged by the guard boat officer. I asked if they could check the time that had been logged on the *Soberton's* watchkeeper's book as I was sure he could verify this. I was then asked if I had checked the *Soberton's* logbook and correctly replied that only the watchkeeper and the Captain had access to it. When the logbook was checked the addition of a fifteen-minute discrepancy meant that my Captain gave me an absolute discharge, much to the frustration of the guard boat PO! The other two offences were not even brought up. I reckoned the Captain was a gentleman of the 'old school tie' who obviously had no time for the devious tactics enjoyed by the guard boat in peacetime. But it was a close shave.

Two weeks later I was transferred to the reserve fleet in Harwich, to another destroyer, the *Milne.* One of the pastimes enjoyed by the crew was spearing the bass which were prolific around the ship's side, feeding on the seaweed that was growing on the ship. A highlight was the fish suppers that we had in Harwich, one of my favourites being skate wings with an enormous helping of chips, costing 6d. We were then told that our ship was to be towed to the Tyne to be scrapped, leaving her with a skeleton crew on board. The tug arrived and one of my first duties was to fit two red glass inserts into the masthead lights to signify that we were not under command and unfortunately I broke them both. The fact that on our three-day tow there was a dense fog was no big deal! Our total complement was a crew of twenty-four - one officer, a PO and the rest ratings. On the first day at sea with a heavy swell on the broadside a pal and I were dishing up when a plate slipped out of my hand and smashed on the deck. My pal said "and another one", and we ended up breaking the lot! After which we had to resort to mugs.

The night before arriving on the Tyne I had been exploring the ship in search of a souvenir and found a locker full of toilet rolls, and with a flash of inspiration I decided to climb the cross trees and unfurl them like the signing of pennants. The next morning the Commander saw them and was not impressed with my farewell gesture and said that unless the culprit owned up the entire crew would be charged. I had to admit it was me and I was given ten minutes to clear it all up, and was also charged, but luckily the whole episode was conveniently forgotten. What I did prove was that the naval issue toilet rolls in those days were far superior to the modern environmentally-friendly recycled ones of today! I was then fast approaching the end of my term of eighteen months of National Service, when we were told right out of the blue that it was to be extended by another six months unless we could give a good reason for being demobbed. I immediately wrote to my mother and told her that it was vital for me to get back to fishing as the *Guiding Star* was now deeply in debt and we were in danger of losing the boat.

I was then transferred to the ship *Abercrombie*, a First World War monitor vessel fitted out for shore bombardment, with a shallow draught and one massive eighteen-inch gun on the foredeck. After I had been on board a few weeks I was escorted to the Captain's cabin by a Petty Officer who had received a letter from my mother. She had written to say that it was vital to have me back aboard the *Guiding Star* as it was heavily in debt, and it was then that the Royal Navy decided that it could finally dispense with me and my dubious capabilities. I must add one trifling incident which occurred when we had arrived at the Captain's cabin and I had knocked on the door and waited to enter. The Captain invited me in and I was followed by the PO and faced the Captain who was sitting in a comfortable easy chair in front of an electric fire. I sat down in the opposite one. The Captain began reading the letter from my mother, which would have melted a heart of stone, and I confirmed that all the facts were correct. The most important one was that the boat was now unable to get a full crew and was about to be sold because of the mounting debt. The Captain remarked that because of the pressing situation he could see no reason for me to serve the additional six months, for which I thanked him and the interview was over. But when we had left his cabin the PO, in a furious temper, said "you had no right to occupy the only other seat when there was a senior officer present - you should have remained standing". I had been interviewed for over half an hour and had told the Captain that my father had been a Captain of a minesweeper during the war and went on to mention that the echo sounder on the *Cleopatra* was the same as on our fishing boat. On reflection, my extending of the interview had really aggravated the standing PO, but I replied "Petty Officer, I am fully aware of that, but when I preceded you into the Captain's cabin, the Captain indicated for me to be seated, otherwise I would most definitely have remained standing, and you would have been seated". I knew that to confirm this he would have to check with the Captain and if it had been correct he would indeed have been made to appear 'petty'. Whether the Captain had done so or not will never be known. The PO just glared at me and the next week I was demobbed. On leaving, I realised that I had thoroughly enjoyed my spell in the Navy and had also made lifelong friends, some of whom I am still in contact with half a century later.

I did learn many lessons from my time spent in the Navy. The first was that discipline is essential in any walk of life, and the second that when occasion demands it is essential to improvise. But because I have an inbuilt rebellious streak and a dubious respect for authority, any further time in the Navy I think would definitely have only been a waste of taxpayers' money. Nonetheless, even now I am convinced that National Service provides the First Lesson in Life for teenagers and makes boys into men.

I arrived back home thoroughly refreshed from my National Service experiences but my father was shocked at my conduct sheet and told me that it was a complete disgrace. I was then faced with reality, a huge pile of unpaid debts for which time was running out. I was facing a very serious situation.

****

The *Guiding Star*

The *Guiding Star* was deeply in debt, like many other white fish boats. My father said we would have to sell the boat and work ashore to pay the debt off. Even at the age of twenty, and fresh from a paid holiday in the Navy, I told him that that was impossible and that the problem was that he had been at the wrong type of fishing for the past two years. We would go back to the herring fishing which we understood but this time recognising the benefit of the echo sounder. The next problem was that for this we would require a complete change of gear - which consisted of a fleet of herring nets, buoys, spring ropes and a variety of other equipment. When we approached the salesmen, and after a meeting in Buckie, they told us that sadly they could not cover us for any further expense. There was no way that I would consider going back to the seine net so I had to fit the boat out for herring fishing in the cheapest possible way. I contacted Cameron of Peterhead who dealt in second-hand drift nets and purchased sixty scrap nets at £1 each, tarred the seine net ropes, scraped together enough second-hand canvas buoys and even used some five gallon oil drums at first. We were now a fully rigged drift net boat.

It was 1950 and we had just begun to fish in the Minch. This was at a time when very few fishermen appreciated the potential of the echo sounder, mostly going by *appearance*, the presence of a whale, solan geese diving and various other indications that there were herring shoals near. One firm belief then held was that the nets had to be shot and set before the sun went down. I knew that if I fished like this my last hope of making a go with the *Guiding Star* was gone, also, gear-wise we had the poorest fleet of nets in the whole fleet of drift net boats. There was no way that I was going to listen to my father's advice of shooting the nets before sunset, on *appearance*, etc. I decided to steam through where the other boats had shot their nets until I detected a shoal on the echo sounder, even if it took until daylight.

Guiding Star sailing down the River Ness passing the
Thornbush slipway

Only then would I shoot our nets. Fortunately for me, and the boat, this did pay off. My father was very concerned about paying off the debt as soon as possible, but my first priority, as I was landing good catches of herring, was to spend some money on better gear. From the Minch we shifted to the Shetland fishing for a few weeks, but due to very short summer nights, the echo sounder not having the same advantage up there, and my lacking local knowledge of the waters, I decided to have a go at the Whitby fishing. My motto was "have gas, will travel". This was the ideal type of fishing for me.

Guiding Star - Avoch harbour 1960 before setting sail for Whitby fishing

Dense, compact shoals with no holds barred and it gave us the boost needed to pay off some of the outstanding debt. Then we returned home to start the winter fishing. This would consist of drift nets at the local Kessock herring fishing and if that failed the West Coast and the herring fishing there.

Pictured aboard their boat in Avoch harbour are the crew of the
Guiding Star who won the Hartley Trophy at Whitby recently for
landing the heaviest catch of herring during the summer season.
Left to right - William Patience; James L Patience;
Skipper Donald Patience (grandad); Robert Jack; George Jack
Patience;Donald Patience; Roddy Sutherland and myself

Left to right - William Patience; George Reid;
Roddy Reid; Frankie Kemp; George Patience;
Skipper Donald Patience

Left to right - Roddy Sutherland; William Patience;
Robert Jack; Donald Patience; George Patience;
Donald Patience and myself; in front James L Patience

Kessock fishing had provided a living for Avoch fishermen for well over a hundred years and up to the 1960's, and with the exception of a few boats from other ports the local fleet had a virtual monopoly of this fishing ground, which for up to six months of the year was in fairly sheltered waters. One of my major inspirations, which I will be remembered for long after I am gone, was the setting up of one of the first private radio programmes, called 'Radio Kilmuir' - in which most of the crew participated. It consisted of a mixture of singing and a repertoire of adverts supplied by me. It had started more or less out of boredom after the nets had been shot, and as many people had the trawler band on their radio we were being received as far away as Edinburgh. This continued for most of the winter fishing and it was just approaching the problem stage of fan mail when right out of the blue the Head Office in Edinburgh contacted me and stated in no uncertain terms that unless Radio Kilmuir ceased immediately our wireless licence would be revoked. To be told this when the Queen was seriously considering me for an OBE - I had heard that even at Balmoral this was their favourite programme - was a real blow. The end to 'Radio Kilmuir' was abrupt and it created a public outcry - and that is putting it mildly. It was evident that someone in authority (obviously tone deaf) was prepared to adhere to red tape and, as the official letter stated, the ships' radio was not for such as this. Thus ended my career as a disc jockey. The post-war period was highlighted by the biggest boat-building boom in history; not the least of which being the demand for ring net herring boats, which for catching the now prolific herring shoals were undoubtedly proving that method to be the most efficient - encircling the shoal, 'ringing', with a massive net about three hundred and sixty yards long and up to a hundred yards deep, heaving up the footrope and getting anything from a few cran (about twenty-eight stone, four baskets) to hundreds of crans in one go.

Guiding Star at prawns in Moray Firth - school
holidays 1967 Crew left to right - William Patience;
Roddy Reid; Frankie Kemp; Arthur Macarthur and myself
in front.In wheelhouse skipper Donald Patience

To compare the drift net method with the ring net is to compare a workhorse with a thoroughbred. This in no way degrades the drift net method as when fishing in open waters out at sea the drift net was far more efficient than the ring net, which depended on mainly surface fishing on inside lochs or in an area where the herring were spawning. The ring net was a very exciting method as one good ring could sometimes provide a week's wages for both crews - possibly two - but much rarer at the drift net where every fish had to be manually shaken out of the nets rather than being brailed on board by the ton. I had been involved in ring netting for a short spell before we had the *Guiding Star* built with a boat we had on hire, the *Budding Rose,* as well as with other boats at different times, but as we could not compete with the more experienced and modern boats we had had little success. When I was demobbed in 1950, as previously mentioned my first venture was drift netting, which fortunately was successful right up to the winter time, when we decided to join two modern Avoch boats the *Heather Lea* and the *Maggie Macleman* for the ring net winter fishing - a partnership which was quite successful but not without an abundance of torn nets as at that time all nets were made of cotton. My biggest problem regarding ring net fishing was that to be successful one had to be patient, which sometimes entailed enduring lying at anchor for days on end waiting for a quiet spell to have a go. Sadly, patience is a virtue which is totally lacking in my make-up (noticeable even in my youth when my father made that comment about the misfortune of having to give me Patience for a surname). Once after a prolonged spell of gales when with our partner vessels we had been at anchor for five days, I decided to leave the partner vessels and go back to drift net fishing - this was against the wishes of the rest of the crew but as usual I had my way. The attraction for me of the drift net was that irrespective of the weather conditions you could always anchor the nets inside a loch and often get a good haul the next day. Another undisputed fact was that the full time ring net men would always be at the top, as there were no short cuts to experience and the knowledge of the lochs and movements of the herring shoals gained over the years by those men. The fact that all too often the ring netters were regarded with envy by the drift net men witnessing these small boats full to the hatches, undoubtedly hastened the birth of the purse net in Scotland. The purse net is basically a massive version of the ring net - whereas the ring net had been capable of catching hundreds of crans in one go, we were now witnessing the purse net capable of catching hundreds of *tons* at a time. So sadly I realised that to be competitive, drift nets would have to be relegated to the annals of history. I was fishing in the West Coast lochs with anchored nets, along with the *Primrose,* without much success, when we heard that back home in the Firth there was a good fishing with the pair trawl for sprats and herring, so I asked the *Primrose* if he would join me in this pair trawl method. As at this time I did not possess a modern pair trawl I decided to leave the *Guiding Star* on the West Coast and go home and improvise a trawl from one of our seine nets and make up a suitable sprat bag from two large bales of sprat netting I had purchased as surplus stock from W. & J. Knox, net manufacturers, in Kilbirnie, Ayrshire

The village hall at that time was ideal for net construction and as I was lacing up the sprat bag, which I decided to make sixty yards long and about thirty yards in circumference at the mouth, a retired Peterhead skipper came into the hall and after one look said "Donald, it's far too big. If you fill it you will never be able to handle it". As usual this advice fell on deaf ears and the following week both the *Guiding Star* and the *Primrose* arrived home to start pair trawling with my converted seine net, and it was only when the net was laid out on our quarterdeck that I began to realise its capabilities. If sprats were easy to catch with this massive bag....... the boats came alongside each other and we

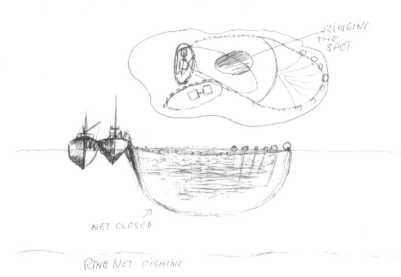

RINGING THE SPOT

NET CLOSED

RING NET FISHING

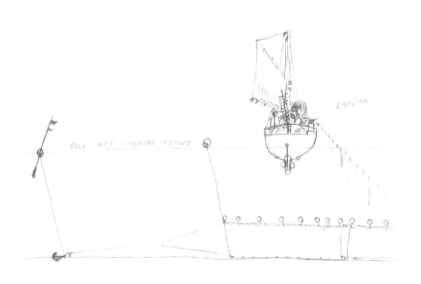

CAPSTAN

GILL NET FISHING METHOD

Sketches by Davy MacLeman artist, poet & retired
marine engineer

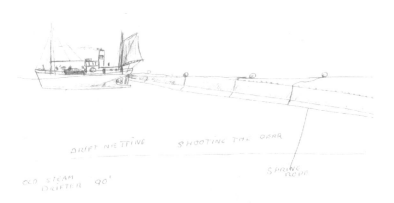

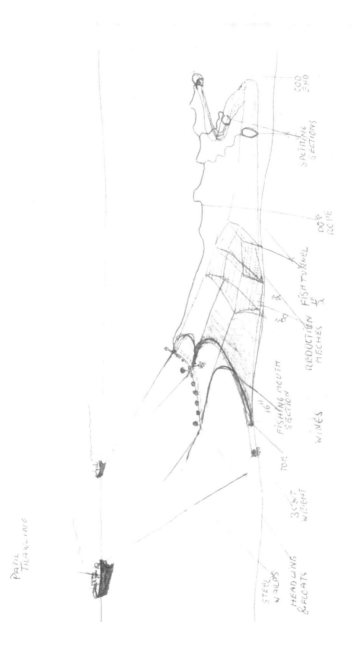

PAIR TRAWLING

STEEL
WARPS

HEADING
& FLOATS

3C&7
WARENT

TOP
FISHING MOUTH
SECTION

16"

WINGS

REDUCTION
MECHES

FISH TUNNEL

TOP
SCOPE

SPLITTING
SECTIONS

COD
END

55

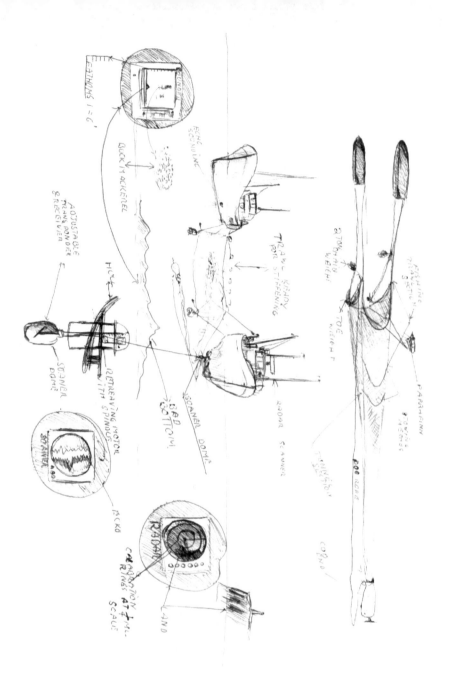

FATHOMS 1 = 6

SOUNDER

ECHO
SOUNDING

DUCK MACKEREL

ADJUSTABLE
TRANSPONDER
& RECEIVER

TRAWL READY
FOR STIFFENING

2 TON/M²
WEIGHT

TOE
WEIGHT

FISHING
TRANSOM
SECTION

PICK

NET WEAVING MOTOR
WITH SPINDLE

SCANNER DOME

SCANNER
DOME

BAD
BOTTOM

SCANNER
DOME

200M
SCANNER

PARAFFIN
TOWING
WEDGES

BOO REEF

TURNING
SECTION

CORD

SCANNER

15CKO

RADAR

CALIBRATION
RINGS AT 1 n.m.
SCALE

LAND

56

steamed the trawl at the east side of Chanonry Point off Rosemarkie where the echo sounder was showing a dense shoal from the surface to the bottom. We had first to spread the trawl, which had a two cwt weight of chain at each lower end, then towed for about ten minutes with twenty-five fathoms of double ropes on each wing of the net, top and bottom. By this time both boats were virtually stopped when astern the bag surfaced - too late for doubts - as one of the crew said "you could play golf on it". I had rigged the bag with four sets of splitting rings, and as at this time it was still floating on the surface we heaved it alongside, tied up the splitting straps and attempted to begin hauling the first section on board in cod end lifts. The *Primrose* had to lash up to my port side as by now the sprats were dead and the dead weight was in danger of capsizing the *Guiding Star*. By the time we had struggled for four hours we had drifted over the reef to the west of Nairn with the ebb tide, and could only salvage eighty crans as when driving over the reef two of the sections had got ripped on the bottom. As usual I had to learn the hard way. Had I gone out on one of the experienced pair trawlers for a day's fishing, I would have learned at first hand that the biggest problem was not the catching of the sprats, but the catching of not too many. First lesson, a sensible size of sprat bag, and in the event of catching too many you run off the first section. By grabbing too many nuts like a monkey you can lose the lot. This method of fishing was to be a life-saver for many boats, as with the demise of drift netting the pair trawl was a relatively cheap method of catching herring, mackerel, and above all at any depth and over any type of ground. I was fortunate in pairing up from the start with one of the cleverest skippers in our village - at that time he had the *Argosy* and I had the *Maureen,* (ex-*Accumulator*) both powered with one hundred and fourteen HP Gardner engines. Sandy also had what I lacked, an abundance of patience, vital in any aspect of fishing. In some ways we were opposites, but it was a partnership that lasted for twenty years.

On my father's insistence I went down to Gordon's College in Aberdeen for my 'ticket' as the *Guiding Star* was over the twenty-five tons limit and, as he told me, I could not depend on his current ticket for much longer. One day when I was at the fish market I went on board the *Ben Lui*, an Aberdeen trawler, and measured his trawl doors. It was then that I decided I would make a scaled down version of them for our boat instead of using the proved ones supplied from the fishing firms. The type of prawn door in use at that time was a light wooden one slung on chains instead of the angle irons used on the bigger trawlers. Later that summer, when we were in Fraserburgh at the herring fishing, the new ferry boat for Kessock was on its way to be launched when it became stuck on the road from James Noble's boat yard to the harbour. As we were tied alongside he asked if we would tow it into the harbour. It took just one jerk and saved them from embarrassment in front of the crowd of councillors from Inverness and the Black Isle - and that was how the *Eilean Dubh* was waterborne. When James Noble offered us payment we refused it as the job had only taken a few minutes, but I could not help admiring some heavy larch planks. They were about two and a half inches thick and I reckoned would make the state-of-the-art trawl doors, and James Noble kindly gave them to me as a gift. They cut them in 5' 6" pieces, three for each door one foot wide, and drilled through them at half-an-inch which enabled them to be bolted to the keels which were two inches by one inch steel, turned for six inches at each end.

When we arrived home to Avoch after our fishing trip I had the local garage weld on half-inch bolts to the centre of the keels in four places, then had the three larch planks bored out, slipped on to them and bolted down. Whilst the welding was in process I was watching so intently and was so totally engrossed in the work that I did not think to wear the proper glasses and was blinded for a few days through my own stupidity.

I think the doors must have been the most expensive set ever made as countless alterations were made to them and nine times out of ten we had a wasted tow. The doors always seemed to lie flat instead of perpendicular and got plastered in mud. After a few wasted weeks I finally had to admit defeat. But suddenly something struck me like a bolt of lightning. I realised what the difference was in the ones I had compared with those of the rest of the prawn boats. Mine were about three times heavier, and instead of being slung on chains, as was acceptable for the light ones, I needed to rig mine with angle irons like the big trawlers. We made straight for Stornoway and arrived in about ten that night.

Once ashore I asked a policeman if he could direct me to a blacksmith and he told me where to go. After my repeatedly knocking at the man's door he finally appeared in a dressing gown as he had been in bed. When I explained to him that this was a life or death issue and that he could charge double time or whatever he wanted, he reluctantly started up the forge and made two perfect sets of angle irons and brackets to fasten to the doors.

The first tow next day, when we heaved up the trawl was ripped, but for the first time the keels of the doors were shining like silver - I could understand the satisfaction all the great inventors experienced throughout the ages when they achieved their goals. Nevertheless, soon after this a Chinese fishing skipper invented 'the steel V door', which was the biggest improvement ever made in trawl doors. It made my achievement seem so small, and not only that, I had robbed a Stornoway blacksmith of a night's sleep.

When I decided to pursue line fishing in 1952, a method of fishing about which I was green, I purchased a fleet of greatlines secondhand from Gamorie, Gardenstown. These lines had one hundred and twenty hooks, about eighteen feet apart, and the fleet of about thirty-six baskets would be over twelve miles long. The bait was mostly herring cut in half, or if small baited whole. One of my crew was an experienced line fisherman and he showed us the basics. The hook was inserted in the head of the herring through the eye and out the back of the head, and the tail half of the hook inserted in around the bone and out the same side. This gave the hook the best grip of the bait and the herring was always cut diagonally rather than straight across.

When shooting the lines the basket was placed on a box at the gunwale, with three men, one aft, one beside him and one on the foreside, so that after a short time it was possible to shoot at almost full speed. The baiting position was the least attractive as in a flap you were the most likely to be foul hooked. This baiting position was mine. In the event of a hook falling out of the cork strip into which the hooks were inserted around the rim of the basket, as sometimes happened, and falling into the line, we always had one of the crew aft of the line and he would then have to grab the line aft of the baiters and hang on to a double bight until things were rectified, as there was always a bit of slack before the line became bar tight. Then if it was pulled out of his hands he was in no danger of being hooked as the loop pulled out, whereas hanging on to a single line it could slip on to the next hook. Despite the fact that as the permanent aftside baiter I had my oilskins ripped with a missed hook time and again, I realise that my father in the wheelhouse had the most nerve-wracking job on board as I kept telling him to go faster, and yet he was always on edge and anticipating the shout of "full astern" when a line became fouled.

The procedure was that the lines were shot before dark in two fleets, with a light on a dahn and an anchor at each end, and depending on your whereabouts – either tied to a pier or jetty or with an anchor dropped for a few hours – you started hauling. If fishing for hake the lines were left all night, for ground fish just two or three hours was sufficient as the bait only lasted a short time on the bottom. The biggest fear at hake fishing was that your lines got trawled away as most Fleetwood trawlers were also after the hake and had the same rights to fish the areas as liners had.

We decided to go fishing on the West Coast for ground fish and the more lucrative hake. Hake always congregated in the deepest holes in the Minch and were a much sought-after fish, fetching about six times the price of cod, skate and other white fish. Before calling at Stornoway for ice and fuel we anchored our nets in Loch Shell on a herring mark and a few hours later hauled them for five cran of herring which we iced down. This was our first attempt at line fishing and I decided to shoot them in the deep water around the Shiant Bank and hauled them for less than a ton of mixed fish as well as the odd large skate which were breaking the snoods. It was obvious to all the crew that the great-lines had seen better days but rather than admit defeat I decided to go further afield and set sail for the Horseshoe Light forty-five miles west of the Butt of Lewis in search of halibut. As we were approaching the Butt the weather had deteriorated to a westerly gale and my father said he was going to bed and to call him on the way back, so I decided to shoot again in the sheltered waters from Cellar Head to Tiumpan Head where we hauled for a few boxes - including one halibut weighing about half a stone - and once again had to watch a few large skate breaking the snoods. I had to admit that the lines were past it and if I were to pursue this type of fishing it would have to be with top quality gear, so I decided to fish with the plaice nets inside Broad Bay whilst being watched by a crowd of locals from the cliff tops. It was on the following day that I found out that Broad Bay was not only prolific in plaice and haddock but was also teeming with large crabs and that the fishermen would only set the fine plaice nets for a few hours at a time. I also discovered that we were faced with two miles of a solid twisting mass of crabs impossible to clear out of the nets, the only way being for two of the crew to jump up and down on them to smash them out and in the process inevitably rip the fine cotton nets. We were able to salvage about half a ton of plaice but the fleet of nets was ruined. My options were now running out so we landed in Stornoway, sold the fish and as a last throw of the dice baited the haddock lines with strips of herring and steamed back to Broad Bay, shot them across the Bay where they immediately floated to the surface with a fish on every hook. The Fishery cruiser arrived and cleared off when he saw us hauling the lines, but the Saint Kilda gulls were having a field day feasting on them and ripping the bellies out. We salvaged over eighty boxes of them, top quality jumbo haddock, and landed in Stornoway only to find that every small boat in Broad Bay was awash with them and that the price had dropped to ten shillings a box. Even in those days that was ridiculous as in Aberdeen jumbo haddock were fetching from two to five pounds a box. I suggested paying the Broad Bay fishermen fifteen shillings a box, we would then gut and ice them and land in Ullapool and, after paying for transport to Aberdeen, at two landings a week it would be a viable proposition. My father remarked "Jack of all trades, master of none, and now that you've proved your point at herring fishing, no more mucking about, so let's get back to what we understand and go back to drift nets". Rather than land our eighty boxes in Stornoway for ten shillings we iced them down, set sail for Lossiemouth, put them ashore for one pound fifty per box then headed for Avoch where the lot was dumped ashore and my ego had its first real knock since being demobbed.

Having mentioned the danger of having lines trawled away, this did happen to half our lines one day whilst hauling off Niest point and our spare gear was in Mallaig. We had intended to head there for more gear when my father said that there was a ship to southward about six miles away with two black balls up. Even with my limited knowledge I knew this was not an 'under command' signal so I told him to head there as it could mean a chance of a salvage. We steamed south and went alongside the *Hugo Heimke Schut* which was from Cuxhaven. She was about one hundred and eighty feet long with a deck cargo of coke built up about six feet above deck level and enclosed with netting wire. I asked them if they required assistance to which they replied "no" - they could fix the problem. I then asked them if they would like some fish and again they refused. Nevertheless I chucked a few cod and ling on top of the coke.

My father suggested we should head for Mallaig for the spare gear as we did not have a large enough catch after losing half the lines. I said no as the wind was blowing easterly at about force three to four and the ship was only five miles off the Hebrides shore, Uishnish Light. As the forecast was increasing to northeasterly, if they could not fix their engine they would require a tow. I decided that we would go back to where we were fishing originally and shoot the lines we had left, anchor there and keep an eye on the ship. It was about seven o'clock in the evening, when she had two red lights up and was drifting closer to the west side, that they began flashing in our direction. As a point of interest, the previous summer whilst we were landing herring to a curer in Stornoway, a Petty Officer with two seamen from a destroyer, the *Crossbow*, which was open for a Navy Day, asked me if he could get some herring for the ship. I told him it would be a pleasure and would a basket be enough. He said that it would be ample and asked me if I could use a piece of rope. I went back to the destroyer with them and he opened a hatch in the stern and hauled out a new coil of eight-inch manilla rope, which needed a local van to transport back to the *Guiding Star*. When my father saw it he said that it was far too heavy for us as the *Guiding Star* was only fifty-seven feet. We kept it as it was buckshee and piled it down the for'ard hatch and tarred it when we were tarring the leader ropes at the start of the season.

When we were making for the *Hugo Heimke Schut* we

pulled up the manilla rope, which I had spliced eyes on, and as we had a length of heavy chain on board, intended for a mooring, which was about a quarter-ton, we shackled this to one end of the rope and the other end to the inboard end with a four-inch bridle fastened to either quarter. On going alongside I climbed the jacobs ladder and the Captain explained they had been unable to fix the engine. He also told me that he thought that the *Guiding Star* was too small to tow his ship and asked me what our horse power was. I realised that to tell the truth, which was only 114hp, would lose us the chance of a salvage so I told him it was 200hp and that we could uprate if necessary. His response was "big power for such a small vessel". He then asked me if I would tow them to Belfast which I said was totally out of the question. So he said it would have to be a port with twenty feet of water at low water, for which Stornoway was the viable option only sixty-two miles away. He then said, looking down at the *Guiding Star* once again, "are you sure you can tow my ship?". I said "as long as you can steer a straight course without sheering about, no problem". He replied "don't worry about my steering - we have electric hydraulic steering. Let's see if you can tow me". We both signed his logbook for the sum of three thousand pounds on the understanding that his ship had to be safely moored up in Stornoway. They passed us a wire through the bull nose which we shackled to the chain, eight-inch rope, and tried to tow her. At first we were unable to move so I told my brother to give the engine button the cold start which boosted up the HP, which should only be used in an emergency. It was enough to get us moving. It was almost nine o'clock and there was about a force three easterly, but the forecast was northeasterly gale and imminent. We proceeded at a steady rate of three knots until we had passed the Shiant Isles, where with a steadily freshening wind and rising sea, we were beginning to lose way and were drifting closer to the shore. The problem was that in the swell our stern lifted high each time and the propeller came out of the water and caused the towrope to slacken. My father told me that unless we called Stornoway for another boat we would lose the ship. I realised that unless we could get our stern down and the prop biting properly he was right. I knew that the water tank behind the wheelhouse was almost empty, so I filled it up with the hose then shut off one fuel tank and filled that up with sea water too, so that all available weight from for'ard was shifted aft to our quarter. By this time we were only a short distance from the rocks, but with the propeller now realising its full potential by virtue of the additional weight aft, plus having the strengthening wind now more on our quarter, we were soon rapidly approaching Stornoway loch. I realised that it was not possible to haul in the towrope manually on account of the 5 cwt of chain in the middle but the ship was dead astern as we passed Arnish light with the wind by then right aft. I told my father to take over the wheelhouse, rushed out and cut the towing bridles on each quarter, jettisoning the tow and leaving us free to manoeuvre. The *Hugo Heimke Schut* slewed broadside on and to my horror was blowing down on Goat Island. I shouted to my father "full speed - go alongside his lee side", which he did instantly, and the German crew, fully realising the danger, passed us a wire rope. I dipped the eye under the stringer then over the timber head, shouted "right-ho, full speed ahead" as we were now both rapidly approaching Goat Island.

There was a sudden crunch and creaking and my father said "we are going to rip the side away". I replied "the strain's on now, don't ease the throttle until we clear the island". No sooner had we done this than the pilot boat arrived on the scene shouting "I'll take over now". I replied "back off, I'm handling this". With the wind in our favour more or less blowing us down to the MacBrayne pier it only required some manoeuvring, tied to the ship, to get him safely moored alongside. No sooner was it done than we were boarded by two Customs Officers asking me if we had had any contact with the ship. I said "obviously - we've towed him, as you can see". They said "did you receive any contraband from them?". I replied that we had had more important things to think about than that - in fact I was less than polite to them, possibly slightly stressed and wound up, with the result that they went through the *Guiding Star* with a fine toothcomb.

Once we had finally arrived at Stornoway and I had told him our real horse power he said that he would not have allowed me to tow his vessel if he had known the facts, but would have dropped anchor until a suitable vessel had arrived on the scene. The Captain had been a Prisoner of War in Scotland and before the war had been captain of the largest ocean-going tug in Germany, the *Sea Bear*. He also gave me advice which I was able to use in later salvage episodes, and that was never to sign the logbook for an agreed sum but to do it on Lloyds Open Form. He explained that all ships world wide carry these forms and if the salvage was completed with one of them a third of the value of the ship could be claimed and also a third of the cargo. His ship was insured for £150,000 which would have meant far more than the £3,000 I had agreed on. I was still very thankful that I didn't lose the ship.

(My father used this information when he later salvaged the Phoenix in 1975 grossing £40,000 for 1 days work).

The following day we steamed south to haul the lines and carried on to Mallaig for more lines we had in a store there. We had a problem in that we required a few hundred more glass balls, which were in short supply. The only ones available were pyrex at 5 shillings each which I considered exorbitant. I tested a glass cider flagon and found that it had equivalent buoyancy to a glass ball. Before I left Mallaig I had cleaned out the four hotels of their empties costing me 6d each. I covered them with netting and once again I was back in business, and 'on the cheap'. In fact the hake seemed to be attracted to Bulmers Gaynor cider flagons. It became a standing gag when we were foul of other line boats, which was common at hake fishing, and other crews saw the cider flagons breaking the surface. The bottles could stand the pressure well and the cider firms were oblivious to their vanishing bottles so I had solved another problem.

The hake season ended after two more weeks so I moved north to the Stornoway waters to fish for ling, cod and conger eel, which were the species that the Stornoway market was interested in. When landing there we knew they preferred the fish to be landed round, 'ungutted', which meant less work for the crew. The German ship that we had towed there was still tied up as it took six weeks before the engine was finally repaired, so every night when we landed we supplied them with plenty of fish and the Captain and both crews became the best of friends. One night I was invited on board by the Captain for a treat of spiced fish cakes which he had prepared specially for me. I got stuck into the first one but one thing I detest is bones, and to be honest it was like chewing a piece of the Siegfried line. The flavour was really good and all the crew were spitting out the bones and thoroughly enjoying themselves. I did, however, get through the meal and congratulated the Captain. This was my first introduction to fish cakes, but being now retired after a lifetime at the fishing, without being boastful I think I can safely say that I have mastered the art of making fish cakes - in fact I could go so far as to state that I will pay £5 to anyone who finds a bone in one of mine.

The day the German engineer arrived in Stornoway with the necessary part to repair the engine on the *Hugo Heimke Schut*, my crew and the German crew all joined for a drink in the Max bar where we were introduced to the engineer, who told me that during the war he had been the captain of a U-boat of the same class as the *Prien* which torpedoed the *Royal Oak* in Scapa Flow. They were regarded as the elite of the German Navy and, as he explained, their only ambition had been to sink as many vessels as possible - on each return to Brest, at champagne parties the main topic was as to who could achieve a 250,000-ton target first. But after one successful trip he went on leave to Berlin to see his wife and family, and on arrival was faced with their all having been wiped out and with only a hole in the ground where his house had been. Only then was the reality of war brought home to him, with awareness of the suffering he had caused and the widows he had created. He consequently suffered a nervous breakdown and could no longer continue as a U-boat captain. The mate of the ship was Karl Black from Heligoland who is now Captain Karl Black, the top pilot there, with whom after all these years I still keep in contact.

As conger eels were fetching a good price, and like hake found in the deepest waters, I decided to shoot the lines back and fore across a trench outside Loch Shell about a hundred to a hundred and thirty fathoms deep. This must have been virgin ground for conger because on the first fourteen lines that covered this deep hole, every hook had a conger or one had twisted itself off and some of them were up to six stone in weight. We only had to lift the deck lids and slide them into the lockers alive, which was easy. The problem that faced us arose when we opened the hatches to the fishroom and found it empty. The congers had prised up the wing boards with their tails, as well as the loose boards in the fish room floor, and over five tons of conger were thrashing about in the bilges - from the stem of the boat through the engine room, cabin, the whole boat. This was the first time we had experienced this type of fishing and didn't know that the top wing boards had to be nailed in, as previously all we had to do was gut and box the fish. Needless to say we had learned the hard way and it took days before we got rid of them.

It was now the early 1950s, when the West Coast had not

yet seen the introduction of the prawn trawl, a venture in which I participated, and one which was a life-saver for fishermen all around Britain. It was also one of the most destructive methods of wiping out our fishing grounds. The reason for this was that for several years we had no restriction in the mesh size used and I have to admit to being one of the culprits who even used a blinder inside the cod end and as a result we completely wiped out the hake stocks. Every fisherman who participated in these first years will remember, both East and West Coast, shovelling out seed hake until there was none left to dump. Because I had line fished for hake this emphasised all the more to me that we were doing irreversible damage to the stocks, and this applied to all other species as well. At that time an average day's line fishing for ground fish, skate, cod and other white fish could be anything from two to five tons of prime fish.

I decided to rig out for lobster after receiving the salvage money as during those days the West Coast boats were doing very well fishing with the traditional pot which was made with a wooden bottom and hazel bows. The one important factor I had not taken into consideration was that the West Coast lobster boats had a maximum crew of three whereas I intended to keep my crew of six - on reflection this was doomed from the start. My crew and I set off for hazel trees, all armed with a new axe, and on our first day cleared out the glen at Drumnadrochit - the next day we plundered the Dores side of Loch Ness as it was my intention to make a fleet of six hundred pots. We made four hundred bottoms - which was just the start. I steamed the hazel in a large old-fashioned washing machine covered with a plastic sheet to contain the steam, which made the hazel pliable enough to shape into bows - then we started making the pots. For a weight we used a dollop of cement and as we had procured a proper cement mixer it speeded up the production. We had already tarred over thirty coils of sisal rope for leaders. My first plan was that I would fish six

69

hundred pots, double that of the Mallaig boats, and thereby solve the question of the extra crew whom I had used for drift and line fishing. I was then facing a very large problem as when we had completed about three hundred pots I realised that this was about the boat's capacity. To carry six hundred pots I needed a much bigger boat than the *Guiding Star*. Something more on the lines of an aircraft carrier would be needed. Our production stopped and the *Guiding Star*, with all the gear on board, looked like a giant haystack - and as the forecast was for a southeasterly gale we had to go through the Caledonian canal. From the wheelhouse the only view was straight ahead and one of the crew had to direct from for'ard until we arrived at the West Coast.

The first trip was an absolute disaster, starting west of Mull, then west of Barra, then the seed reef where we had our first narrow escape and on to the Flannel Isles and another close shave. By this time my father had had enough and told me that he was going ashore at the end of the trip. We tied up at the pier in West Loch Tarbet alongside one of the Mallaig boats at midday on the Saturday and alongside an experienced lobster fisherman who asked how we had got on. I told him we had eight cases which we had anchored off the pier. He asked me if I'd broken the nerve in the claw, which was something new to me, so I told him that we had tied the claws with twine, and it was then he told me that if one of the rackings became loose that lobster would kill the others. He showed me how to do it by inserting a small screwdriver in the joint of the crushing claw, thus immobilising it. We left the pier, lifted our cases and as the first lobsters were large I bent the screwdriver. The next screwdriver was a bigger one and as I was in charge of this operation I completed it in record time. The following weekend we landed in Mallaig, to be told that with the arrival of a new buyer the prices were at a record level. But a catastrophe had occurred - by inserting the screwdriver too far I had killed most of the lobsters. To try and solve this problem I got rubber bands, but after another trip I realised that to keep my crew I had to revert to pursuing drift and line fishing as it was impossible to make lobster fishing viable since I lacked the knowledge that the West Coast men had gained over the years. When we finished the next trip, coming through the sound of Harris I tied up at the pier at Leverburgh and asked the local fishermen if they were interested in buying my fleet of creels. I sold them all for £1 each, with thirty coils of rope slung in. I think I must have been a most unpopular skipper, and quite rightly so as the crew had to see eight weeks' work chucked away for nothing. I realised that whatever lay ahead for me I was not cut out to be a lobster fisherman.

The weekend was what, for all fishermen, made it worthwhile, especially where the younger ones were concerned. When the last basket of herring or fish was landed, fishroom and boat scrubbed spotless, the next on the agenda was number one. Most fishing ports were fortunate to enjoy the facilities of a Seaman's Mission where you were always assured of a welcome and could enjoy the luxury of a hot bath or shower, etc. Then, rigged out in your clean gear, all the fraps of the past week were soon forgotten. Owing to the restricted space on fishing boats in those days, your shore-going clothes were kept in a suitcase at the end of your bed, and when kitted out in those the world was your oyster. The highlight every Saturday night was going to the local dance hall - in Whitby, the Spa Ballroom. I must admit that whilst for dancing I would never win any trophies, with the help of some "false courage" I usually had a go. In the Spa one evening with a friend of mine, Hugh Patience, I said "Hugh, I fancy that lovely blonde girl over there" and Hugh said "well, have the guts to ask her for a dance", which I did. This was to change my life for ever, and now, 45 years later, I am still trying to come to terms with how fortunate it was for me. After that dance I escorted Maureen home and arranged to meet her the following day, in the hopes that she really would arrive at the place we had agreed on. From then on I was in love for the first time in my life and after a successful courtship we were married the following year – Maureen has been my stabilising factor ever since.

She decided to marry a Scottish fisherman who was, as I realise now, suffering from an exalted ego, to put it mildly, and in later years said "I have had the misfortune to marry a nylon miser, gear takes preference to everything". Even the local salesman said "Donald, you have spent more on gear this year than all the fleet in Avoch combined, screw the bobbin."

I was still adamant in pursuing line fishing and whilst in Whitby I was told by a Whitby pal of mine, Bob Pennock, whom I had met in the Navy on the *Cleopatra*, that a local fishing company who owned five fishing boats, the shipyard and Eve's Garage at the docks, had rigged out three of their boats for line fishing for halibut in Iceland the previous year but the venture had been unsuccessful and they wanted to dispose of the gear. I met Mr Eve with my father and he confirmed that he wanted to get rid of the gear stowed in the forty foot loft above the garage which was filled to capacity with mostly brand new lines, Italian hemp ones which were the best available in those days, dhans, anchors, thousands of rigged hooks - all a line man's dream. I asked him the price for the whole lot and he said fifty pounds, which I told him was ridiculously low, but to close the deal he would not accept more than a hundred pounds as he was only too glad to clear the place out as he had further development plans for the area. I was now in a position, gear-wise, to go line fishing anywhere from Rockall to the Faroes but I realised that the *Guiding Star* at fifty-seven feet was too small for deep-water fishing. This was in the early fifties when the big 'liners' were among the most successful fishing boats in Britain, catching top quality fish like halibut.

An important feature of the herring fishing at the Yorkshire grounds at this time was that dense shoals of cod also arrived on the grounds, feeding off the herring, and as the Yorkshiremen were among the first to perfect the bobbin trawl for hard ground fishing for the smaller type of boats in Britain, it was a common sight to see those boats arriving in virtually awash with cod - full to the gunwales. One day when fishing off Scarborough and landing there, I witnessed one of the finest displays of fish landed by a local line boat, the *Progressive* - massive cod and an odd skate, all laid out in the market - caught from Baymans Hole, about thirty-five to forty miles off. One of those cod was on display as a tourist attraction, weighing out at over twelve stone. Some holiday-makers were admiring the catch at the time and when a group of them stopped at a large skate one remarked to the others "that one's got a right bash", obviously thinking it was a flattened cod. Scarborough suffered from one major drawback compared with Whitby, which was that it did not have the benefit of the river Esk which flowed through Whitby harbour, where once at the market you could discharge at almost any time. Scarborough harbour dried out until the next tide, which brought all landing to a halt. When in Scarborough with the ebb tide, you had always to ensure that your boat had a list to port, towards the quay, which was emphasised one day when the harbour had a large fleet there and the boats were in tiers of six or seven off the pier. The outside boat listed, pulling off the next, and it ended up with all six boats lying on their beam ends hard against each other with most of their gunwales smashed up in the process. The danger of further damage was avoided on the next flood by the liberal application of heavy grease to the bilge of each boat to prevent the broken timber heads doing more damage when the boats hopefully slid back up against each other, which they did. Nonetheless, this resulted in five of the boats ending up with extensive damage to their topdecks and afterwards they all moored separately to the quay, with ropes ashore rather than tied to the adjacent boat. The uneven contours of the harbour bottom, often caused by boats' propellers blasting holes when manoeuvring with both flood and ebb tide, were the reason for problems such as this.

The next few years were mainly a combination of herring, line and increasingly, prawn fishing, which meant that the Minch was becoming less viable for line fishing. The pattern of Avoch fishermen was mainly West Coast in the summer and the Kessock herring in the winter in local waters.

My first attempt at cooking was when we ran out of bread at the lobster fishing, west of the Hebrides at the Monach Isles. We were at anchor at the time and with the rest of the crew asleep in the cabin I found a bag of self-raising flour, plus butter, sugar and eggs. Thus began a hobby which took hold of me more and more, until in later years I combined the jobs of cooking and skipper and did both. One period when drift netting at Shields and I had a crew of ten, it was my practice to go aft to the galley while the crew were hauling the last few nets and fry up a quick snack for them - usually sausage, bacon, eggs, beans and anything else I could lay my hands on. But one particular morning when I asked them what they fancied one of the older members of the crew said "what about porridge?", something we had never had on board, and this request was backed up by the rest of the crew. With all my previous experience in cooking this was a first for me as I had been sickened with porridge as a youngster and to my knowledge it hadn't been included in our stores since I had purchased the boat the previous year. On searching the large food lockers I discovered an almost empty packet of porridge oats left by the previous owners but by no figment of the imagination was it sufficient to satisfy ten men, so I added a large packet of cremola pudding, half a pound of butter, six eggs, a tin of carnation milk, some water and boiled up this concoction. When the crew arrived aft the member who had first requested porridge exclaimed "What in the name of heaven is this? I've been forty years at sea but never seen yellow porridge before!" I said "this is Vitamins A, B and C, get it down you". Strange as it may seem the food of a mighty race was never again on my menu. There were of course times that combining skipper's and cook's jobs inevitably resulted in a less than perfect end product, but on the whole it functioned well enough and I told the crew that anyone who was not satisfied could take over the cooking - but there were no takers!

Once when we were trawling off Barra Head on a Sunday (I always made a special effort on Sundays) I was deeply involved in baking a special cake into which I had put the contents of a tin of mixed fruit. This was cooking happily in the diesel stove, but when cleaning the control valve I must have accidently turned it full on as a short time later when I was in the wheelhouse with one of the crew we heard an almighty bang in the galley. The stove was red hot, the oven door blown off, and my creation covered with soot. The rest of the crew were still asleep so I told the crewman, as I was in the process of cleaning up the cake, not to tell anyone what had happened and said we would call it 'explosion cake'- it was enjoyed by all.

After the fiasco of that cake I decided to concentrate on more basic types of cooking, and considering the fact that half the world have rice as their staple food I thought I would try my hand at rice pudding. I was fishing in conjunction with a Fleetwood trawler, the *Boston Sea Hawk*, and we were both stormbound in Castlebay one weekend. So, thoroughly bored, I decided to make a special rice pudding for both crews and have it ready for their return from the local pub on Saturday evening. I boiled up bulk rice with currants and stuck a large dish in the oven, then joined the two crews for a drink. Once back on board I insisted that all hands would have to partake in what was by now a colossal rice pudding, done to perfection. The following day when we were towing off Barra Head the

Boston Sea Hawk was still in harbour - apparently most of the crew were suffering from some mysterious symptoms which had baffled the local doctor. Their limbs had seized up, and the two of the crew who were fit had to take the boat to Mallaig. On Monday we received information via one of my crew who said that when the doctor had tried to take a blood sample from one of the *Boston's* crew the syringe was choked with rice. This was a total exaggeration, as anyone will realise, in fact it was only said in jest, but from then on I realised that rice is cooked in ounces and not pounds. I have to admit I learned another lesson in the art of cookery.

On another occasion, when I was pair trawling for herring and landing to the klondykers at Ullapool, my crew were hit with a bug that caused sickness and diarrhoea so I went up to the local chemist to get something to clear it up. The chemist shop was very busy at the time and he told me to go through to the back of his shop to discuss it in private. He advised me to check the dishcloths because if the cook was using dirty ones that could be the cause of the infection. I told him I was the cook as well as the skipper, and that I was more hygiene-conscious than St Bartholomew's Hospital - I was using about a gallon of parazone a week for dishcloths, toilet, sink and other areas. He replied that this could well be a contributing factor. Parazone?? Anyway the bug vanished after two days and my crew continued to flourish on my basic type of cookery and I reckon my galley in modern times would be considered E-coli free!

One winter's night when we had anchored our nets in Loch Shell through heavy marks of herring, I decided to make a batch of scones to pass the time before hauling the nets. The crew had been yarning in the cabin and when I presented them with the still warm scones said that they were the best yet - the entire batch was consumed in no time. I smiled and looked at my hands which were now spotlessly clean; little did they know that I had been splicing the tarred ropes prior to baking. Privately I wondered if this could have enhanced the flavour?

I recall occasions when, with my overriding confidence in the capabilities of the *Guiding Star*, and my own pigheadedness, I was very fortunate not to have been 'lost with all hands'. Once, when we were approaching the Pentland Firth and making for the West Coast during a strong breeze, we received a weather forecast at midday which was giving out force ten NW imminent. My father told me to make for Scrabster until the weather improved and I said "forget the forecast" as we had a new boat. By the following morning it was force ten off Cape Wrath and suddenly we were struck by a massive sea on the starboard shoulder. The boat lay over on her beam end so far that the oily bilge water burst up between the panelling and the outer skin, hit the deck head and ruined the two top beds on the port side of the cabin. It also burst the skylight open which resulted in some flooding. We finally arrived in Stornoway ten hours later with a shambolic cabin and with another lesson having been learned by me.

Some time later when we were having poor line fishing in the Minch, I studied an old Close's fishing chart which marked halibut on it on the edge of the Continental Shelf from February to April. This was about fifty to sixty miles west of the Hebrides, and I decided it was worth investigating. My father's response was that the chart I had been studying had been printed over thirty years earlier and was out of date for fishing information, but this fell on totally deaf ears. As usual, I had my way. It was now February and the boat was on the small side for Atlantic fishing during the winter months. Nevertheless I was determined and we set off. It was whilst cutting the bait, herring, which was always cut in half in readiness for shooting, that my father said that the echo sounder had packed in and we would have to head to Mallaig for repairs. I went to the wheelhouse, altered the depth setting and found that we were out past the edge of the Continental Shelf in two hundred and eighty fathoms of water. So I decided to steam back a few miles and carry on shooting the lines on and off the edge of the shelf to a depth of eighty and a hundred fathoms, which was where the halibut were shown on the chart. After about four hours we began hauling the lines and straight away the first line had a good mark which we thought were porbeagle sharks. This particular species was then very much in demand for the Italian market and even though we were catching cod and barndoor skate too, in comparison with porbeagle these were 'rubbish' fish. The halibut were non-existent, but as porbeagle were still prolific my father told me to dump the barndoors as he thought we would make a more lucrative catch with the sharks. I decided to cut off the wings of the barndoors, which was the norm, as they weren't entirely worthless. Eventually, when we finished hauling that evening with more than two tons of shark, all shelved and iced, and with almost the same amount of cod and skate wings, the forecast was increasing to a northerly gale force, so I decided to steam in closer to Barra Head and shoot the lines about twenty miles off the Head instead of making for the market as my father had suggested. We shot the lines, dropped anchor with a few coils of heavy drift net rope and set the watch, one hour each until the next morning - only to be faced with a full gale. When we heaved up the anchor it was shining like silver as we had unknowingly been dragging it all night over the sea bed. Once again I had made a bad decision and it was only after punching through the gale for nearly three hours that we eventually picked up the first dahn. After hauling another three lines we found no fish but encountered a broken end. The weather was getting too much for us so we set off for Mallaig to land the porbeagles with the rest of the catch and to take on board our glass floats. This was very much like hake fishing and could also be beneficial for porbeagle fishing but on the way back out we still had to retrieve the rest of our lines.

Next morning we discharged our catch on the quay with all the crew sworn to secrecy about the location of the porbeagle as we wanted to use our knowledge of it for our own benefit and have at least a few days' full-time fishing by ourselves. It was only when the salesman and the buyers arrived that I was informed that what we had thought were porbeagle were in fact large tope and so we would have to take them back on board and dump them as they were totally worthless. This was in the early '60s and I realised then that line fishing was becoming out-dated and prawn trawling was the best alternative for my class of boat.

I have previously mentioned that when I was demobbed from the National Service I was confronted with the fact that the *Guiding Star* was so deeply in debt that the salesmen, after a meeting, decided that they would cover us no further for alternative gear - and also told how after that my gamble with the second-hand herring nets paid off. Later I went completely overboard, as this next episode will show. It was common knowledge that Broad Bay north of Stornoway was one of the richest fishing grounds in Britain for plaice and haddock and for this reason was well watched by the Fisheries cruisers, and from the seashore too. Plaice nets and lines were the only methods that could be used there legally so we commenced rigging about two miles of them and I purchased some second-hand haddock lines. This was before nylon and courlene came to the fore and only cotton and natural fibres were used. The haddock lines consisted of hemp line and the snoods to the hooks were made from horse hair. To get the raw materials I went to the knackery at Alcaig on the Black Isle where I was given a sack of horse tails buckshee and the man in charge assured me that he could guarantee an unlimited supply in the future and would appreciate a fry of fish anytime. To further implement this expedition my father, on my advice, purchased a second hand fleet of great lines and I told him we would also take twenty five herring nets to anchor which would enable us to catch our own bait for the lines. By this time, with all the gear on board - two miles of plaice nets, thirty baskets of great lines, twenty-five drift nets and fifteen haddock lines - the *Guiding Star* was more congested than Noah's Ark when the last animals were boarding, and to suggest that I was suffering from an acute bout of gear-mania would be putting it mildly, as well as a bout of over-confidence. As one of the crew stated, "you would need hiker's boots to get fore and aft on this bitch". To say that it was a fiasco would be an understatement and I won't dwell on it. The one lesson I did learn, however, was that the great lines correctly pursued could provide an alternative way of fishing to help fill the slack period.

Once when we arrived in Stornoway I was told that the *Windfall*, a large steel drifter, was going to be sold and Duncan MacIver, the owner, who also had a business in Stornoway and was a personal friend of mine, told me I could have the vessel for four hundred pounds, which was the scrap price. It still had the steam engine but as she was in tiptop condition and grants were available for conversion at that time, I was desperate to buy her. My plan was to install two one-hundred-and-fifty HP Gardner engines on a twin gearbox, which was feasible, but my father reminded me that the *Guiding Star* was only four years old and told me to forget about the *Windfall*. The *Windfall* was without doubt the best-maintained steel drifter in Britain and, as Duncan had told me the previous year, he had had the decks completely renewed with Oregon pine from Canada, which must have cost a fortune. She had the same Echo Sounder and WT as the *Guiding Star* and only required new engines to convert her from steam to diesel. Duncan told me that he was confident that the boat would pay but sadly she was sold to Holland for four hundred pounds, was converted and fished successfully for many years there. My father, as a consolation, allowed me to purchase the entire fleet of herring nets, over a hundred, all top line gear, before the vessel was sold. Maureen and I had been married for a few years and our son Donald and daughter Jacqueline were by now three and four years old. We always looked forward to the Whitby fishing as it enabled Maureen to spend some time with her own family, a break thoroughly enjoyed by us all. It was common practice with the fishermen since time immemorial to whenever possible have their families join them as they followed the herring shoals. This year in particular I suggested to Maureen that if she were willing, instead of travelling to Whitby by train, which at that time entailed four changes, they could go down in the *Guiding Star*, which would take about thirty-two hours' steaming. We left Avoch with plenty of herring nets, as you had always to be prepared to lose nets when the prolific shoals struck, and with Maureen and our two children plus all their luggage for the season. My father did his utmost to prevent my taking the family down by boat and was all too soon proved right, as after a few hours the weather had deteriorated - there was now a strong north-easterly wind blowing and Maureen and Donald were suffering all the traumas of sea sickness. It was also clear that no way would they be able to endure the claustrophobic atmosphere of the small cabin with its noise of the adjacent engine.

Behind the wheelhouse we had a large cage for stowing the buoys which I roofed over with the hatch cover and a large tarpaulin, then put a layer of spare drift nets on the deck of this enclosure and added a wandering lead with a light fixed to the roof. This was the best I could rig up for the family, but at least they were kept dry and had plenty of fresh air. Thankfully, after clearing the Moray Firth and heading south past Aberdeen the wind dropped and the rest of the voyage was made in dense fog. Nevertheless it was a

October 1955

Bumper catches bring net losses

WHEN the Scots' herring fleet returned to Scarborough harbour on the morning of October 1, many of the skippers were complaining about the current glut of herrings which was causing heavy losses to their fishing gear, particularly the nets.

One skipper said: "On moonlight nights the herrings swim lower in the sea to escape the light. So our nets have to go down to about 18 fathoms and they need extra 'strops' (bands of rope) to do so.

"There is an abundance of herrings just now and the heavy catches, plus the weight of the 'strops', are making many nets split.

Last night, the Ugie Vale, of Peterhead, shot 22 nets and 17 of them split. The Guiding Star, of Inverness, shot down 22 nets and 20 of them split."

FRUSTRATING WORK ... Donald Patience, right, and Donald Macleod, crew members of Scots keelboat Guiding Star, repairing damaged nets on the North Wharf, opposite the King Richard III House

Scarborough Evening News
Donald Patience and Donald Macleod mending nets on
Scarborough North Wharf

82

lesson well learned and never again would I suggest they came with us - had the weather kept deteriorating the outcome could have been much worse. After this experience they always made the journey by train. This brought home to me in no uncertain way what young women had had to endure in the past when the sailing herring boats were all too often their only means of transport to the various herring grounds where they gutted the herring caught by their menfolk - all too often in the worst possible conditions, and for a mere pittance - this being their only means of support.

One particular day that always sticks in my memory was in the summer of '52 whilst we were steaming from Ullapool, along with five other driftnet boats, making for the Handa grounds off Cape Wrath. We were inside the boat when crossing the deep water off Loch Inver on a beautiful calm day in June, at about four o'clock in the afternoon, when one of the crew saw a strange creature with a head on a long neck, at least three feet long, above the surface. I can only describe the head as being similar to a seal's, but much larger and having that distinct neck. We decided to attempt to lasso it and I and one of the crew each made one, then we slowed the boat down and approached the creature to within a few yards, but both attempts missed and it dived down, giving us all a clear view of its body. The creature was about eighteen to twenty feet long, had large flippers, one on each side, a grey/brown/black body with a white blotch on its side. It reappeared on our port side and as before dived under again on being approached. In all we made four or five attempts to catch it, and the nearest boat on our offside, the *Marguerite*, called us up on the WT enquiring if we had a man overboard as we had been circling so much. My father reassured him that all was well and then told us to forget what we were trying to do as we were only wasting our time. Catching herring was what we should be interested in. This I well understood was our main priority, but to this day, forty-five years later, I have never had any enlightenment as to what the species might be. Compared with the Loch Ness monster, towards which I have always had a very cynical attitude, this was a real creature which had been observed by all the crew. I am by nature a cynic, or was until some years back when the *coelacanth*, considered to be a prehistoric species which had died out a few million years ago, was caught off the coast of Africa very much alive. That creature we saw was no Loch Ness monster, or whale, or walrus, but it did convince me that where the oceans depths are concerned there are still many unanswered questions.

On a lighter note, on two occasions when line fishing, the first time in Rhum Sound when we were having good fishing of roker skate, we saw two skate coupled together in the sex act - as one of the crew said, "they are prepared to lose their lives for it". The other occasion when we saw this was in the deep waters off the Tiree passage when we hauled in two large blonde roker in like circumstances. As one of the crew had a spring balance he weighed them both, one was twenty-two pounds, its partner eighteen pounds. It is apparently a not uncommon sight, but in all the years of line fishing these were the only two occasions we came across it. I was told by some Whitby fishermen that when they had been line fishing for turbot in the past it was a common occurrence to witness other turbot swimming up to follow the one on the hook, and by leaving that hooked one in the water they were able to gaff the prospective suitors on board. The record for this was held by the *Endeavour* WY, who were able to gaff ten or more followers on board before finally taking in the hooked one. As I have never fished for turbot myself I can only state the facts as we saw them - perhaps they strengthen the long held belief that skate is an aphrodisiac?!

One day with a severe westerly gale I was towing away up the Sound of Sleat with a friend of mine, skipper of the *Golden Ray*, off Isle Ornsay, when I saw what I thought was the Fisheries Cruiser coming north around the Point of Sleat towards us. I contacted my friend and said "I see the cruiser, Luie, heave up" - he said "you're okay, Donald, I've been told it's not the cruiser". I thought he had been given the all clear from other prawners further south. I told my crew to relax and continued towing away and shortly afterwards we became fast; when this happens I always shut off the wireless transmitter and concentrate on heaving back until we can break the gear free. But this time, just when I had shut it off Luie realised it *was* the cruiser and was repeatedly shouting to me "it *is* the cruiser, heave up Donald," to which I was oblivious. We were in the process of hauling the trawl with a decent lift of prawns and skate when the cruiser, *Brenda*, appeared at our stern shouting on his loud hailer for us to stop for boarding. This was a foolproof case of illegal fishing, but I told the crew to shovel the lot overboard while I kept circling to keep the wheelhouse and galley between us and the *Brenda*. After circling round a few times with the cruiser following us and repeatedly shouting "stop your vessel", I stopped the boat when all evidence was jettisoned, and the captain of the *Brenda* told me to follow him into the shelter of the bay behind Isle Ornsay lighthouse to be charged. He dropped his anchor and I tied alongside and climbed on board with my ticket and the boat's register, realising that this time I was in for the works unless I did some quick thinking. I entered the bridge where Captain Henderson had the chart for the Sound of Sleat on the chart table with a cross indicating where he said I had been apprehended. He said "I am charging you with illegal fishing where we observed you hauling your trawl". I replied "you are charging me with nothing at this point" - my mind was still not functioning properly. He then said "I have a crew of twenty-one to verify this". Right out of the blue I said "what you saw was my crew gilsoning the trawl up with the power block whilst repairing it as it's far too heavy to handle manually, and had you been alongside during the last few hours you would have observed this happening several times". His next question was "why when I told you to stop your vessel did you keep circling round?". I said "at the time I was in radio contact with the *Valiant* who was towing off Barra Head to ascertain if it was fit for fishing in the South Minch weather-wise, and was only circling around whilst I was debating whether to proceed North or South". He continued to look at me whilst tapping his fingers on the chart and I said "what is more to the point, Captain, is that my crew are suffering from a throat infection and we have used up all the medicine in the First Aid cabinet and I would be grateful if you could give us something to help us". A silence followed, so I left his bridge and found two of his officers on board my boat measuring my gear with my crew standing beside them on the deck. To my surprise the Captain now also came on board with a large brown dispensary bottle which I sampled first then passed it to one of my crew who said "cheers", spluttered, and then said "what in the so and so is this?" I said "it's for your throat Roddy", as he had mistakenly thought it was rum, whilst at the same time thanking Captain Henderson for his generosity. Another factor that could have caused me a problem was that when I told my crew to chuck all the catch overboard they had thrown the live skate down to the fishroom, and when the officers went down one of them slipped on the heap of still flapping live skate. Thankfully this was not mentioned and a few months later I was fined £25, just for undersized mesh, and cleared of the major charge of illegal fishing. Captain Henderson was a gentleman of the old school as this must have been one of the most cock-and-bull alibis that he ever listened to - possibly giving me Brownie points for ingenuity.

When I reflect on the post-war years before modern technology was taken for granted - decca, radar, auto pilot etc - the echo sounder and wireless transmitter were the be-all and end-all for us. Lighthouses were a vital aid to navigation for all fishermen and Stevenson, who built most of them, especially in Scottish waters right up to Mukkle Flugga at the northern tip of the Shetlands, must have saved many lives from shipwreck. He must have been one of the greatest engineers in history in this field and most of the lighthouses still stand after all these years - though now mostly automatic - as fitting monuments to his memory. I can still recall the many lighthouses with their equally important fog horns and the vital part they played in navigation for all seamen of my time. The West Coast of Scotland, unlike the East Coast of Scotland and England, had only occasional days when you became fogbound, but at those times how glad we were of the blast of the foghorn to guide us to safety. I have always regarded gales and storms as the acceptable norm, but in those years before decca and radar became part of every vessel's equipment, fog was our biggest fear. The Whitby herring fishing was where I had the privilege of meeting my partner in life, Maureen, and on four different occasions I won the trophy for the top catch of the season, the Hartley Cup, and it was there we encountered the most fog. All too often the blast of the foghorn on Whitby Eye Lighthouse and the siren at the pier end, with the clanging of the bell buoy at the outer end of the reef, would last for days on end. While steaming out of the harbour in those ghostly fog-bound conditions, when even the pier ends were hardly visible, you always set course to the nor'ard to clear the reef on the south side until out past the bell buoy. Once out in the North Sea the pantomime began when the fleet encountered the shoals of herring located with the echo sounder - all too often this was in the shipping track of merchant vessels whose courses passed a few miles off Whitby Eye Light. With a combined fleet of Scottish drift and ring net, English drift netters, plus at that time Dutch herring luggers, it was mayhem on a massive scale - all chasing the elusive silver darlings. The fact that no lives were lost in the occasional inevitable collision says a lot for the seamanship of all concerned, and there was always a great sense of relief when you crept in through the pier heads the following morning, where everything had a ghostly appearance in the fog – hopefully with a decent catch aboard.

I was towing away at the prawns with the *Guiding Star* one Saturday from inside Rhum to Eigg in foggy conditions when the boat came to a virtual stop - obviously we had picked up a large boulder or boulders. We were unable to heave up the trawl to our quarter, so I had to tow it into the beach at Eigg to attempt to empty the cod end. This process of towing it into the sandy beach took about two hours as we were only creeping ahead - eventually, about midday, we ended up at the shore in two fathoms of water. Whilst heaving up the bag I was going slow ahead to try to stop the trawl fouling up the propeller - but just as the cod end was breaking the surface the propeller gave a thud and the engine stopped; the rubber footrope was in the propeller. We restarted the engine out of gear, and as we were immobilised I contacted the salesman's office in Mallaig for one of the boats to come out and tow me ashore. They assured me that my pal Luie of the *Golden Ray* would be there in less than two hours. The immediate problem was to attempt to empty the cod end which, when heaved to the surface, we saw had a good haul of prawns with two large boulders underneath. Visibility was at this time about one hundred yards and we were shovelling out the prawns above the boulders through a hole we had cut in the bag when out of the fog the Fishery Cruiser *Stroma* appeared and shouted on the loud hailer that they were arresting us for illegal fishing. I told them forcefully that we were fouled up, that I had been towing the trawl ashore for the last eight hours from out in the Minch and that Oban radio could verify this - also that I suspected our gear box was smashed up. They immediately volunteered to tow me across to Mallaig, which offer I gladly accepted. When the *Stroma's* crew were passing the tow rope the captain said "what's the skipper's name?" On being told, Donald Patience, he said "well he hasn't got much patience". After about half an hour the skipper of the *Golden Ray* called me up saying that the only boat he could see was the Fishery Cruiser *Stroma*, so I explained that it was towing me but that he could now take over. Thanking the captain of the *Stroma* for his help, Luie then towed me into Mallaig where two of the crew of the Taits' purser the *Conquest*, with their diving gear, cleared our propeller. When steaming back out for the evening tow my uncle said "what if the Fishery Cruiser is still there?" I replied "well lightning never strikes twice in the same place".

Another episode concerning the local Kessock herring was once when the shoals disappeared prematurely and we thought it was an ideal opportunity to let the engine on the *Guiding Star* have its annual refit at Lossiemouth - which we did, but no sooner had we done so than the elusive shoals appeared again. To commence fishing with the local fleet we decided to take out a small skaffie belonging to the local hotelier, about thirty feet long, whilst the *Guiding Star* was overhauled and painted. Our dog, Teddy, a black Labrador which had been on the *Guiding Star* from the age of six weeks, and which my father had said would have to be left ashore as there was no room for him on the skaffie, was locked in our net store until such time as we should have left the harbour. However, when we were fastening the nets in the harbour Teddy appeared at the boat and leapt on board. When finding himself locked in the store he had broken through the window to once again join the crew and follow his natural way of life. The fo'c'sle on the skaffie was tiny, consisting of a small bogie stove for cooking and bunk beds either side - this was adequate for our basic needs but as every man had his week's food in a rectangular box known as a *kistick* and headroom was about four foot six, it was impossible to have Teddy there when we were dining. My father, who always sat directly under the small open hatch, was having his supper as we all did on a plate on his knees when Teddy, obviously in his own way of showing disapproval of not having been included, performed an unmentionable act which landed on my father's plate. The dog was fortunate in not being consigned himself to Davy Jones' Locker together with my father's supper. Though the others considered it hilarious, even my father later saw the funny side and made sure that Teddy was included at meal times in future.

The practice regarding transport to and from the West Coast in the post-war years was for crews to hire a bus to take them home and back each weekend from the different fishing ports - Mallaig, Gairloch, Ullapool, etc., until by the late sixties most had their own transport. When five or six crews were travelling on the same bus the stragglers were a continual source of 'aggro' as everyone was eager to get home.

One particular Saturday from Gairloch five crews were together in a Newtons' bus - these being from our boat, the *Guiding Star,* and four other Avoch boats, one of which was the *Heather Lea.* When leaving Gairloch, just up the glen from the harbour I saw a fantastic carpet of bluebells among the trees on the lefthand side and on impulse asked the driver to stop as I knew that Maureen, my wife, would appreciate a bouquet of them. As anyone who has gathered bluebells will know, there always seems to be a better selection farther on - however I finally had a lovely bunch and it was only when arriving back at the bus and one of the crew of the *Heather Lea,* Andrew, said "nice bluebells, Donald" and I replied "yes, and there's plenty more if any of you want them". It was then I realised what the rest of the crews' priorities were as regards bluebells. When I had initially asked the driver to stop, as happened quite often, usually for someone to answer a call of nature and relieve himself as there were no toilets on buses in those days, this was quite acceptable.

But I soon found out that horticultural expeditions were definitely taboo. Needless to say it was all taken in good part and Maureen thoroughly appreciated the thought as this was at the time that our son Donald was born.

Avoch herring fleet – Whitby 1969
Skipper of 'Heather Lea' Andrew W Macleman in front

Avoch herring fleet - Scarborough 1969

Avoch fishing fleet –Scarborough1969

I sometimes wonder if a similar circumstance could have led to the birth of Interflora as it is a coincidence that soon afterwards it became a worldwide concern, "say it with flowers".

I once became involved with telephone cable laying - at a time when I was prawn fishing with the *Guiding Star* on the Nairn grounds in the summer of '58. As you could only catch the prawns at night in those shallow waters, the Avoch boats were mostly landing at Inverness and selling to the factory at Bunchrew, with the result that they were tied up at the quay all day. One Tuesday when I arrived at the Thornbush to land our prawns, we saw a small puffer with an open steel skiff alongside and a crowd of men arguing on the pier. One of them was a friend of mine who was employed with telephone stores in Inverness and I asked him what was going on.

He told me that the puffer had been hired to lift a cable to enable them to repair any faults, or alternatively to lay a new one if it was beyond repair - but, as he explained, "the puffer is hopeless for the job, it's been one cock-up after another". First, when they lifted the cable, which had a buoy at either end - one at the Inverness side and another at Ardturly Point on the Black Isle side - the plan was to drop the cable into a large snatch block fastened to the stem of the puffer, then steam slowly along whilst the cable slid through so as to spot any damage, and then heave that part on deck to repair it. This first operation had been a fiasco, "as I've said, Donald, the puffer has not got enough power to pull your drawers down", then when it had attempted to tow the steel skiff and lay a new cable across, the ebb was on, and instead of going straight across, both the puffer and the skiff were swept down the Firth, resulting in this shouting match on the quay. I asked my friend Joe who was in charge of the operation and he told me it was a Mr Brown, an-ex naval Commander, whom I later found out was one of only three survivors who spent 14 days in an open lifeboat after being torpedoed in the arctic during the war, from which ordeal he had suffered severe frostbite. Joe also advised me "whatever you do, Donald, don't argue with him as he flies off the handle very easily". So being pre-warned I approached him quietly, being aware that he had told the puffer skipper that they were "finished", and said to him that I was certain that my boat was capable of doing the job. He agreed to this suggestion and immediately told his men to transfer their equipment from the puffer to the *Guiding Star*, part of which being the large snatch block which was then fastened to our stem. We steamed out and picked up the buoy at the Inverness side, heaved up the cable and put it into the snatch block (the cable was about 2" in diameter) then steamed along it slowly until a damaged piece of it was located. To then get that part on board we had to fasten a nylon rope to it and heave it on board with the aft gilson derrick, then lay it on the deck lashed fore and aft on either side. With it now secured they commenced to strip the outer covering, a thick tar-like tape, then came a lead cover and inside umpteen strands of copper wire. After a few hours' work the repair was completed, having all been done under a tent on deck - I presumed this was to keep it dry. Our only involvement was keeping the squad supplied with tea and sandwiches, and, as I had been warned, not in any way to upset Mr Brown. About 5 pm the cable was released and I landed them all back at Inverness, but I was told they would leave their equipment on board overnight in case the cable was still faulty and a further repair have to be done.

We set off for the prawn grounds, arriving at the close, and both tows resulted in a good night's fishing - about 35 stone of tails - and on Wednesday morning after landing them Mr Brown and his team arrived again as, he informed me, the cable was still faulty. Purchasing two dozen pies and the same number of tea cakes from the shop at the Thornbush, as there were about 20 involved including myself, we set out and repeated the operation and another damaged part was spotted about 50 yards further on from the first repair. So it was basically a repeat performance of the previous day, again landing them at Inverness then having our two tows, this time for 30 stone - still O.K. Landing the prawns in the morning, the team arrived back yet again - the cable was still faulty, and as Mr Brown explained "we will give it one more go today" - which suited me perfectly. This time I doubled up on the tea cakes and pies, set out and repeated the performance, landing them again around 5pm. On Friday morning when we landed the prawns, Mr Brown and his team arrived once more and said "it's no use, we're going out now to jettison the cable, which means lifting it at both ends out past the low water mark, cutting it then leaving it". By this time I had found out from my friend Joe that there were six other cables also laid there, which would mean that it would be impossible to try later to grapple and salvage the faulty one - I had checked up with a scrap merchant about the estimated value of its copper and lead and he told me about £3,000 as at that time the price of copper was through the roof. I said to Mr Brown "I will salvage it for you for half the scrap value, but once you cut both ends it's gone forever". My reasoning was to no avail as he said "I'm in charge of this job, not you", and when I then suggested that they at least leave the floats on the ends he completely flew off the handle, and things were only made worse when I said "have you the authority to waste this?". It was only afterwards that my friend Joe explained to me about the Commander's having being torpedoed during the war and just six months after our encounter he died. But after arriving back at Inverness on this final occasion we discussed the payment for the operation and I said £150 a day for the 3 days, to which he said "that's ridiculous, you were only involved for a few hours each day and it never interfered with your fishing at night". I said "Mr Brown, when I agreed to do the job I was prepared to work any hours you required and as your equipment was on board for 3 days I was employed for that period" - to which he finally and reluctantly agreed.

In the immediate post-war years the stocks had had the benefit of the six years of the war to build themselves up, and the waters around the UK were literally teeming with fish. I remember one occasion at the great-lines when we shot the fleet from Dunvegan to Canna for ground fish and on some lines were hauling up to twelve barndoor skate with an average weight of one to two cwt. This catch was the heaviest haul we had ever encountered and it meant having two men to back up the line hauler as it was like lifting trawl doors. When each barndoor skate surfaced we had to clip a strong steel gaff into its head and with a handy billy (block and tackle) haul it up to the gunwale, where we would cut off the wings and then dump the carcass. When we eventually finished hauling for the day we had about four and a half tons of wings and about the same amount of cod, skate and ling - the biggest haul we had had so far. I decided to shoot back in the same area, this time for a total catch of about one ton, but this time there was not a single barndoor skate to be seen. I was told later by an old experienced line fisherman that you never got a second day's fishing in the same area for barndoor skate after you'd dumped the carcasses - another lesson to remember.

The only market at that time for barndoor skate was in France, for the dog tracks, but a good market could give as high as seven shillings per stone. The largest barndoor skate that we landed in Mallaig was one that we caught at the Stoer Bank and this was before we had started winging them. It weighed out at thirty-six stone and had nine hooks stuck in its mouth, in different states of corrosion, which one of the crew said was like Goering with medals. The price we got for this leviathan was thirty-six shillings. The white fish levy at that time was one shilling per stone and the carcass was dumped. These giants of the sea have been fished to near extinction and sadly I have contributed to this state of affairs.

I can think of no other method of fishing more in tune with nature than the traditional drift net. Witness, at sundown, a fleet of drifters riding head to wind with their mizzen sails set - once upon a time in every direction - this must have been the most tranquil and natural way of catching herring. The only sounds to be heard were the clucking of the St Kilda herring gulls that congregated around the drifters' sterns and an occasional whale blowing off to windward (followed by the foul smell of its breath). It was common practice for the man on watch to fish with the dandy at this time, usually having six to eight hooks about six inches apart and a lead weight at the bottom, a 'jigging' type of fishing. The most welcome news from the man on watch for the rest of the crew was "they are playing solid all around us now." This was part of the natural movement of the herring shoals; a bottom fish in daylight hours, rising to the surface as darkness approached, and in those pre and post-war years before fishing had advanced to its present-day state they could be heard leaping out of the water in their countless thousands. No-one can turn the clock back as progress is inevitable, but the ever-present danger is that we are fast approaching a stage where technology is quite capable of wiping out the stocks, already proved at the Newfoundland Banks, to name just one area.

The method of line fishing which I found achieved the best results was to follow the ring net boats on a Monday and get the week's bait off their first ring while the herring were still leaping aboard. Twenty-four baskets were sufficient for four days' fishing and eighteen of these were packed in tin trays with a lid tied down and buried in a locker of ice - this ensured top quality bait. The other six baskets were cut up ready for the first shot. When fishing for hake each line had to be kept off the sea bed, as explained previously, by the addition of glass floats spread along the line and a weight at each line end. Hake being a much sought-after species, and as one box of hake was worth at least six boxes of cod or other fish, this was a much-pursued type of fishing, always in the deepest troughs in the Minch. It was always very interesting to try out another deep trench in the hope of hitting the jackpot, a haul of hake, the only problem being that if there were no hake there we hauled the lines with the bait still on the hooks, whereas if ground fishing you were almost certain of ending up with a fair day's work, which could vary from two to five tons of mixed fish. Another problem we encountered in some of the deep areas when mostly fishing for ground fish was finding prime fish reduced to skin and bone by flat, red, centipede-type insects that we called bees. It was one of the most soul-destroying sights for any line fisherman to haul in large cod, or other large fish, and then when they hit the deck see these vermin pouring out of empty carcasses. These areas could be fished for hake without problems as the hake lines were being kept from ground contact by the glass floats. One of the attractions of hake fishing was that the lines fished for a much longer time as the bait was clear of the bottom and the vermin, and as most of those deep areas were within short steaming distance of some harbour or jetty you could moor there in safety for the night.

The times when we shot the lines to try for hake across a long narrow trench south of Loch Skipport then tied up for the night at the small jetty there, we were always assured of a welcome from the local people and it was a much-appreciated break to be invited to their homes for a couple of hours and then when leaving to be give a biscuit tin of freshly baked scones. It only requires the smell of a peat fire for those memories to flood back after all those years at sea, and for me to appreciate how fortunate I was to experience the welcome those people gave us everywhere in the Hebrides - from Barra Head to the Butt of Lewis, in Skye, Canna, Coll, Tiree and in fact everywhere on the West Coast. It went a long way to alleviate the hardships of fishing.

During the post-war years and right up through the sixties, times when restrictions were kept to a minimum and freedom of the seas was the privilege of every fisherman, my philosophy was "have gas, will travel". One week in particular, which for a 114 hp vessel must have been an all-time record, was whilst drift netting, beginning with the first shot on the Monday off Barra Head where we hauled for a few crans. Then, as I knew that there was good herring fishing at the Douglas Bank off the Isle of Man with the ring net boats, I set off for there, arriving on the Wednesday night at where a fleet of ringers were filling up their boats. We shot our nets through a dense shoal of herring - the echo sounder was black from top to bottom. It was my first time there, and after a short while we started hauling the nets which were very heavy-fished, but the sea was literally boiling with massive dogfish that were having a bonanza grabbing the trapped fish from our cotton nets and ripping out pieces of them in the process. To say that this was a disaster would be to put it mildly. They were coming on board tangled up in the nets and the deck was soon awash with them. Fortunately we had only shot twenty-five nets and we hauled these in hell-for-leather, ending up with forty-five crans on board and most of the nets ruined, plus having had a large percentage of the catch chewed up by those shark-sized dogs. What I found out afterwards was that the ring net boats, when they tied up the net to the herring bag which was made of heavy twine to save the bag from the dogfish, had two of the crew, one fore and one aft, continually chucking out herring to feed them until the catch was on board. I realised that this heavy-fished ring net fleet had more than ample to supply the Isle of Man and that my chewed-up catch would be less than welcome there, so I decided to land in Ardglass in Ireland. On arrival there a buyer came down to our cabin, shook hands with me and told me that he would buy our catch for £3 per cran if I would sign on with him for the season. As he also gave me £5 for a drink for the crew as a goodwill gesture, I readily agreed.

I landed the catch in bulk to a lorry where they salted them heavily in preparation for curing. Irrespective of my having agreed to this contract I realised that it would be suicide to pursue this method of fishing. There was also the fact that closer scrutiny of our catch showed it would not live up to the buyer's expectations, especially after the dogfish had fed on it. So after discharging it and hearing that there was a good fishing at the Whitby grounds, I set off right away for the Forth and Clyde canal, which at that time was still in operation, arrived there on Friday morning and entered the first lock. The canal at that time was badly silted up and my father who was in the wheelhouse was steaming dead slow, and when I repeatedly told him to speed up he said the boat wouldn't steer if he went any faster. To which I in my ignorance replied "rubbish" and took over the wheelhouse and at the first bend in the canal we ended up on the bank, almost hitting a bus passing on the roadside. However, we eventually emerged at the Forth end, having literally scraped the bottom most of the way and with the propeller throwing up a dead cat from time to time. This was for me one of the most nerve-wracking days I had so far experienced and the sense of relief when we finally cleared the canal and were back in the sea was tremendous. I had had visions of the *Guiding Star* being stranded halfway across Scotland. The canal was closed the following year. We arrived in Whitby that Saturday evening to begin one of the first and most enjoyable herring seasons of my life.

Whitby will always be remembered with nostalgia by all the Scottish fishermen who through the years participated in the herring fishing, as the friendliness of the local people and the holiday atmosphere generally was for many the highlight of the year. This was a completely different herring fishing, where a massive concentration of boats

100

would be steaming about the grounds in the evening with the echo sounder right up to the close showing no indications of herring, until suddenly the sea would become alive with them and the echo sounder black from the surface to the bottom. Drift net fishing in most other areas in Scotland, east or west coast, normally required shooting the fleet a fair distance away from other boats, usually no less than a few hundred yards, but at this Whitby fishing very often only the width of the boat governed the distance apart as everyone tried to get a shot through the shoal, and this inevitably resulted in massive tangle-ups. The herring seemed to strike the nets in such quantities and so quickly that it was common practice for some boats to lose the lot within minutes as they were pulled down by the weight of the fish. One advantage this kind of fishing had for Avoch fishermen was that it was very similar to the Kessock herring fishing that we had at home, where in the narrow waters of the Beauly Firth where the herring were concentrated in very confined areas this was how we fished. The only difference being that if the nets went down there it was in shallow water with a soft sandy bottom and you could normally haul them up, whereas at Whitby fishing when they went down they were in Davy Jones' Locker, full stop. Another governing factor at that fishing was the way the herring reacted to the moon as it waxed. They would cling further down nearer to the sea bed and to catch them we all had to lengthen our buoy ropes and sink the nets to the top of the shoal. This caught them okay but when the boats' fleets became entangled it was pure mayhem. One of the worst situations that we could encounter was if the fleet drifted foul of one of the large Dutch luggers, as their fleet of nets could extend for about one and a half miles and were always rigged for near-surface fishing, so if one were using long buoy ropes, from 10 to 15 fathoms long, their nets were in a different stream of tide. This was a situation to be avoided at all costs as the Dutch luggers salted their catch on board and could spend weeks at sea. Time was not important to them whereas the UK boats landed their catches daily.

One particular night, while searching for a suitable mark on the echo sounder, I ended up among the Dutch luggers where I picked up a good mark between two of their fleets which were using short buoy ropes, three fathoms long, and as from the tip of the mark it was about sixteen fathoms to the bottom, I decided to shoot about thirty nets between them with fifteen-fathom buoy ropes, knowing full well that I would inevitably become foul of one of them. This was a one-off incident, never to be repeated, as we had to tow every net from under the Dutch fleet of surface nets, in the process wrecking most of my nets which were heavily fished - and undoubtedly doing the same to the luggers' fleet. Nevertheless, when we hauled up the Dutchmen were only starting to haul, about a mile astern of us, so I steamed away as fast as possible. When the moon was full the spawning herring were drawn down to the sea bed, which was all hard ground and were virtually impossible to catch with drift nets, but we discovered that above those marks there would often be a swim of herring right at the surface, where it could only be detected as tooth marks, and just for one or two fathoms down. This I learned from a Whitby skipper - as he told me, "when they are hard down, fish the surface".

Towards the end of the season the approaching winter made its presence felt, with the odd gale confining the fleet to port and the shoals having spawned and vanished once again into the open waters of the North Sea. When stormbound with northerly or northeasterly gales you were always fortunate to get up through the bridge, which was opened on a cantilever system, and get into the safety of the dock away from the surge of the sea at the market area. Whitby by this time presented a completely different picture as the holiday season was now over and the holiday-makers, like the herring shoals, had vanished once again. The amusement arcades were all closed up, stalls and souvenir shops shuttered until the following season, and to the howling of gale conditions, it was now time for the Scottish fleet to head for the relatively sheltered waters of the West Coast or the Inverness Firth. The pattern of the Whitby herring shoals was for them usually to appear at the start of the season around Skinningrove, north of Whitby, then gradually shift south of Scarborough until they vanished somewhere in the region of Flamborough Head. Yet at the end of the season it was still possible for an occasional shoal to turn up once again at Skinningrove and I was prepared to be one of the last to leave the grounds as the fishing here for us provided a good financial boost.

The wreck of the *Guiding Star*

Monday, 5th December, 1963 was a typical stormy winter's day. As we arrived back in Ullapool after the weekend at home I had a throat infection so was not in the best of form. I decided that with the Christmas tie-up period approaching we would leave the West Coast and end the year at the Kessock fishing at home, in sheltered waters. A big point in favour of that Kessock fishing was that our boat would be in complete safety over the tie-up period, whereas on the whole of the West Coast north of the Clyde at that time the only secure harbour able to accommodate a large fleet of boats was Stornoway.

The Kimara FR178, Skipper Charles Duthie, ashore in Loch Broom, Ullapool Loch after hurricane of 1982 - all boats refloated successfully.
(dad's advice to me always have a 'rope ashore' – never leave your boat at anchor)

Guiding Star in her safe berth - Ullapool harbour

All too often extensive damage faced many who had left over this period. Ullapool harbour, one of the busiest ports at this time, was very exposed to southerly and southeasterly gales and the majority of the East Coast fleet had either to anchor or to tie up at moorings in the loch. Both options carried a problem in that unless two of the crew remained on board, the boat was not covered by insurance. As one can imagine, after a week's hard fishing there were not many volunteers for that. We left Ullapool that Monday evening for the Pentland Firth, along with the herring fleet who were steaming out to resume fishing. The weather conditions were now approaching gale force, with occasional snow flurries, and the six o'clock forecast was giving severe gales. However, as the wind would be stern-on as far as Cape

Wrath, then offshore all along the north coast to Duncansby Head, by which time hopefully the weather would have improved, I decided to turn in for a few hours and set the watch. After a short time in bed - by now north of Ullapool and with the wind and sea blowing us ever further northwards - I had just dozed off when one of the crew on watch woke me saying that the drift net fleet were having heavy fishing off Loch Ewe and a Buckie boat, the *Amethyst*, was calling me up on the WT offering me some of his nets to haul as he already had his quota on board. Fishing at that time was restricted to forty crans per boat, about seven tons, as the market was limited. I said "forget it" but a few minutes later the crewman said "you had better come up and at least talk to the skipper", which I did. The skipper repeated that he had his quota on board but that he was quite prepared to hang on to the rest of his nets until I arrived back south to haul them, rather than have to shake them out and shovel the fish overboard. Dumping herring back into the sea after shaking them out is one of the most soul-destroying experiences for any fisherman. I thought "well another day won't make a lot of difference" and much against my better judgement I turned back south into what was by now a full gale, arriving alongside the *Amethyst* some two hours later. Hoisting the mizzen sail in preparation for hauling the nets, without which it is not possible to keep the boat head to wind, it was becoming increasingly obvious to me that once again I had made the wrong decision for the rapidly deteriorating conditions. But I had committed myself by then as we had begun to haul the nets which were loaded with herring and the *Amethyst* was already on her way to Ullapool. My crew at that time was a total of seven and I was the youngest at thirty-three. The mate was in his fifties and the rest were all over pension age, including my old uncle at seventy-two, retired for a few years but having obliged me by coming aboard to stand in for one of the crew ashore at the time.

After hauling a few nets I was having increasing difficulty in keeping the boat head to wind as with the now severe gale, the snow and the *Guiding Star* literally standing on one end and continuously falling over on the broadside, the nets, of which we still had about twelve to haul, were by this time, instead of being hauled, merely see-sawing back and fore. Having to cut away another boat's nets after accepting them is for any fisherman the utter humiliation; but by this stage we had no other option as with the snow and spindrift visibility was virtually nil. I reluctantly told the crew to cut away the gear, whilst I tried to hold the boat head to wind - no easy job as to cut it away entailed cutting the heavy leader rope and also cutting through the nets full of herring. By this time, as I had been unable to hold the head to wind, we were mostly broadside with decks awash. When we hit the cliffs off Priest Island I was using full throttle and the boat swung around after the first smash - the nets and the leader rope fouled up the propeller, stopping the engine. The crew rushed aft to the galley where I told them all to put on their lifejackets, one of which was in each bed in the cabin, and after sending out the Mayday I climbed up to the galley roof where the inflatable life raft was kept in a container. I now saw the reason why I had been unable to hold the *Guiding Star* head to wind. The mizzen sail had blown out of its ropes and was in shreds. By this time the boat was stern on to the seas, caused probably by the drag of the gear around the propeller whilst smashing against the cliffs on the starboard side. I managed to inflate the life raft in front of the wheelhouse with the crew holding on to it, as to launch it would just have it burst like a balloon between the boat and the cliffs. So I said we would have to keep it on board until the last moment, as the boat was obviously sinking though still surging along the cliff with the heavy seas. One of the crew was still down in the cabin, my old uncle. I went down to where he was sitting on the cabin seat up to his knees in water filling his pipe with black twist tobacco. When I told him to get up on deck immediately with his lifejacket he said "Donald, don't try to fool me, I've been too long at sea to realise that there's no hope for us. I intend to meet the end in comfort down here". Nevertheless I got him up on deck along with the others before the lights went out when the engine room flooded. By now the stern was under water but the heavy seas were still surging the wreck ahead. We dragged the life raft further for'ard but meantime, unknown to me, when the lights went out one of the crew had leapt onto the cliff off the starboard side. The boat was finally brought to a halt with its stem against a ledge from which I was able to pluck the crew off and from where we scrambled up the cliff and behind the edge to comparative shelter. Then I found we were one missing. We were now in hurricane-force winds and blizzard conditions, and I told the crew to crawl around in a search, keeping close together, whilst I went down to the wreck to try to find the missing member. The wind was so strong that I had to force myself down the cliff, where I encountered a soft object in the water. My first reaction was that it was his body but I then realised that it was actually the remains of the burst life raft. Another order which I had given the crew earlier was to remove all surplus clothing, as at the time I was certain we would all end up in the sea. This order most of them had thankfully disregarded, and I was the only one who had stripped down to jeans, singlet and socks. The fact is that we were wrecked at the peak of high water, and judging from the final resting place of the *Guiding Star* the tide must just have been on the ebb. Had the boat foundered sooner we would all undoubtedly have lost our lives, but in its dying throes it stopped at the only place on the south west corner of the Priest where we could have disembarked. I grabbed some of the 60" plastic buoys that were floating around me, tied them together and literally got blown back up the cliff to find that now all the crew were accounted for, and that the greatest danger facing us was hypothermia. Behind the cliff we huddled in a hollow where I first slit open their lifejackets and padded them with the kapok, myself included, then scraped up any available heather or ground - and we all ended up covered with this. And for those with no headgear I cut open the 60" plastic buoys to fit over our heads, together with a lining of kapok. Could this have been a vision of today's Tele-Tubbies?

Thus began the longest night of my life, which ended at daylight the next morning with the arrival of the *Rosehaugh's* crew who had landed on the inside of Priest Island and travelled across to where we were pitted like potatoes. As one of that crew said, "they burst out of the ground like a covey of grouse". The Priest Island is roughly one mile square, surrounded by cliffs with a small loch in the middle and with what we saw at daybreak to be the walls of a ruined house close by. Another boat, the *Silver Reward* BCK, was also wrecked that night at about the same time, but fortunately struck the north west corner of Priest Island where the crew were able to get into the life raft and were blown up the loch where they were rescued by another boat, the *Narninia*. At the height of the storm that night a wind force of one hundred mph was recorded by the fisheries cruiser in the vicinity - it ended the life span of the *Guiding Star*, three times winner of the Whitby trophy for the highest catch of the season. The following week three of us went out to the wreck with a dinghy towed out by a launch from Ullapool, to row ashore and see if it was possible to salvage anything at all. We were faced with a tangled, smashed-up wreck. My only regret afterwards was that I could easily have unfastened the steering wheel which was still intact on the empty deck, and taken the trophy that was still on top of the mast. I was cleared at the following enquiry held in the Custom House in Inverness by an officer of the Board Of Trade from Aberdeen, a Captain Skinner, attended by both my mate and myself. Apparently, using the kapok with an additional covering of ground etc. for insulation was considered to be in my favour, and most important of all was the fact that all the crew were saved. One of the effects I suffered from the wrecking was back pain which was later discovered to be a dislocated disc. I realised that to regain my confidence I had to get back at sea as soon as possible.

The Wreck of the *Guiding Star*

The fishing vessel *Guiding Star* of Auch was wrecked on the rocks of Priest Island near Ullapool on the night of the 6th December 1963. There was a tempest raging at the time and nothing could be done for the helpless and stricken craft, as her propeller was fouled by nets and the night was as dark as the grave. Her crew of eight Auch men had a miraculous escape from drowning, and but for the mercy of God, the village of Auch would be a sad village indeed.

They were fishing for herrings around Ullapool Bay
Till the herrings got scarcer and scarcer each day
And now he was steering his proud *Guiding Star*
Young Donald the skipper, well-known near and far.

He'd decided this day to sail his boat home
Decided long last no further to roam
But fate had decided no harbour she'd see
And so, as they say, it just had to be.

She steamed from the Bay ere daylight was born
Not waiting as others another day's morn
Ploughing the billows as homeward she sped
With her crew unaware of what lay ahead.

Her hatches were battened and covered full well
To help her brave better the sea and the swell
On ever on northward she steered
But the sun never shone and the sky never cleared.

Young Donald by fate was turning her round

Heading again for their old fishing ground
To try once again for the 'Scattan' galore
But the wind it was strong, when the nets were put o'er.

Soon they were hauling for high were the seas
And into a tempest was mounting the breeze
As wave upon wave now over her bowled
Her faithful propeller got suddenly fouled.

She shuddered and shook but great was her strength
Braving each wave which struck her full length
Upward and downward she reeled and she lifted
And into the darkness, all helpless she drifted.

She wallowed in foam, she thudded full loud
The rocks she had struck, and the crew were knee bowed
Ere her wheelhouse got washed, they say to the beach
The mate, her transmitter, was able to reach.

Gasping for breath his message got through
Of the loss of the boat and the plight of the crew
But the village of Auch was stricken with fear
And some prayed aloud and some dropped a tear.

There were cliffs by her bow and cliffs by her side
And but for God's mercy they'd perished and died
For rolling and rocking she stuck on a spot
The safest, they tell, Priest Island has got.

They clawed at the rocks on hands and on knees
Dragging the injured. soaked, washed by the seas
Dragging the men in the darkness of night
Desperate men, with land in their sight.

Soaked to the skin on Priest Island shore
Safe from the seas and the billows' loud roar
But what of the boat, the proud *Guiding Star*
She'll sail nevermore for the 'Scattan' afar.

James Jack

111

Maureen Days

I was fortunate in getting a berth on board the Avoch ring net boat, the *Aspire*, which partnered the *Rose - Abie* and Sandy, two top-line fishermen - when they fished first at the sprats in our local waters then went to the herring in the West Coast lochs - ending up in the Clyde where my back problem was so painful that I had to come ashore for treatment. After a six weeks' course of treatment at Raigmore Hospital in Inverness I ended up wearing a corset contraption and thought I was fit enough to resume fishing. However, once a skipper you are never content until you are back in the wheelhouse, so when the *Accumulator* FR came up for sale by public auction in the Dalrymple Hall in Fraserburgh I was determined to buy the vessel. At the final bid, which I understood was mine, I went up to the auctioneer to close the deal, only to discover that an Irish fisherman had outbid me by £200 - a genuine mistake, but legally I had lost the boat. However George Alexander (Dodi), the owner, intervened, saying "it's my decision; Donald's bid gets the '*Accumulator*'". A Macduff-built boat, and a decision I remembered forever - the best break in my whole life fishing-wise. I was fairly soon to re-name the boat *Maureen* after my wife.

My intention had been to resume drift and line fishing, but by now these methods were becoming less popular and required ten of a crew, so I rigged out for prawn fishing which needed only about four. The conversion work was done at the Macduff Boat Yard - a trawl winch and Gibson derrick. Taking the boat from Fraserburgh to Avoch with a westerly gale, after a sudden lurch I was once again in agony with my back problem and arrived in Avoch harbour like crippled version of the Hunchback of Notre Dame. I told my wife, Maureen, that I had the boat but was going to be useless for fishing unless I could sort my back out, so it was back to Raigmore where the surgeon told me I would have to have an operation. A friend of mine had had a similar problem which had been rectified by an osteopath in Edinburgh, so I told the surgeon that I had just purchased a boat and would try the osteopath first. His response was that he would not put his worst enemy to one of those bone-setters. The next day I made an appointment, went down to Edinburgh and was strapped to a traction bed, which to me made sense as it was similar to a winching operation. He located the disc, told me to hang on and pushed it into place, then told me not to do any heavy lifting for at least six weeks, and as far as the corset was concerned, to dump it in the bin. His fee of three guineas was the best investment of my life.

Maureen INS 215 leaving Avoch Harbour - 1968

We arrived at the West Coast grounds and shot the trawl in a force six breeze. It was then that I discovered to my dismay that over the broadside the boat was rolling gunnels under and one of the crew remarked that one would need six legs to balance on this bitch. I realised that to work the trawl, rigged as we were, we needed ballast - as compared with a drift net rig-out which entailed weight-wise at least ten to twelve tons of gear with nets and leader ropes. I called up the salesman's office in Mallaig and asked if they could have eight tons of road chips waiting on my arrival, which I thought would solve the problem. The chips were enough to fill four side lockers each side half full, and with a false wooden top we could still use them if needed. Which did solve the problem for the time being - until I could have the bilges cemented. But that would only be done if this was to be my future type of fishing.

The first summer at the prawns from West to East Coast grounds was really not what I had been used to. It seemed to me more-or-less a scraping method of fishing and lacked the excitement of herring fishing. The winter Kessock fishing, however, provided me with a boost. The next summer I decided to return to the drift net herring fishing with the *Maureen* and a full crew of ten. Even if that meant turning the clock back it was my decision. We started off on the West Coast from Barra Head to the North Minch and it was apparent, even to me, that the purse net and pair trawl had an adverse effect on the once prolific shoals, so I shifted North to the Lerwick grounds. I encountered a similar situation there, hauling one Tuesday morning north of Foula and close to a Fraserburgh boat called the *Incentive*. The skipper asked me if I had heard the news from the Shields grounds about the LT drifter, the *Wiseman*. He was always the first to start the Shields herring fishing as he could expect record prices for small catches. Donald Patience, the skipper of the *Incentive*, was a cousin of my father's and had heard on the ship's radio, as he understood it, that the *Wiseman* had landed twenty-eight crans of herring the previous day at £30 a cran. This immediately lifted me from the doldrums and as my motto was "have gas will travel", I did.

On the Thursday morning I called into Berwick to refuel, arriving off the Shields pier-heads in the afternoon, where I decided to wait until the *Wiseman* put to sea. It appeared fairly soon and I called up the skipper, whom I knew personally, and asked him where he had caught the twenty-eight crans on the Monday and also about any further landings he had had since. Albert, the skipper, informed me that the so-called twenty-eight crans were a myth as he hadn't caught twenty-eight *herring* in the last month. Obviously the news that my namesake had heard was incorrect. I decided that there was no point in lingering there so I called up one of the WY whitefish boats to see if they had any information about herring in the North Sea and a KY boat responded and told me that the Dutch trawlers were getting good fishing at the Devil's Hole. I located the area on the chart and on arriving there with no signs of the Dutch fleet and with the echo sounder as lacking in life as the surface of the moon, I realised this was another wild goose chase, so steamed north and arrived in Wick on the Saturday night. We sailed again on the Sunday for another go at the Minch grounds with a slightly demoralised crew, which was emphasised when I overheard someone saying that he would need an oil tanker following him.

When we decided to return to the East Coast I was just able to keep the crew together until the Yorkshire fishing began in August. We were hauling a very heavy catch off Skinningrove and luckily a Customs friend of mine was on board for a fortnight's holiday. He was armed with a bottle of distillery whisky which he had kept for such an occasion as reviving the morale of the crew. It must have been at least 200% proof, and rather than merely reviving the crew they ended up rolling with laughter and I had to hand over the nets to a Fraserburgh boat. This was the fishing where I once again won the WY Trophy and we returned to the West Coast winter fishing where one of our main markets was the Dutch klondykers, who salted the herring. This was before the appearance of the Eastern Bloc klondykers who arrived on the scene when the purse and pair trawlers finally made the ring and drift net obsolete. A new fishing was emerging around this time. It was prawn fishing. Before this period of fishing they had been thrown back as rubbish, but because of advertising cookery programmes on TV they soon became a delicacy and proved to be a lifesaver for the smaller class of ring and drift net boat.

Scottish fishermen have by nature always been individualistic, a characteristic probably strengthened by the Highland Clearances two centuries ago when people were forced out of their crofts when the lairds decided to replace them with sheep - this all too often having the backing of the local minister. Thousands of families were shipped out to the colonies like so many cattle, but for those who remained the beaches were their only resort, resulting today in fishermen who are capable of competing anywhere in the world, given a level playing field. The latter sadly all too often nowadays being denied them. The rest of their problems have evolved from the inevitable reliance on policies dictated by politicians in Westminster, who for the last century have done nothing to further the interests of Scottish fishermen, as countless delegations who continue to return from Westminster empty-handed can verify. I experienced this personally over twenty years ago when I was one of a delegation of 370 skippers who went down there to demand a 50-mile fishing limit for Britain. For all the genuine interest we were shown we could as well have been talking to a crowd of Martians. I addressed one MP, Lord Mansfield, and listed all the countries in the world which had the benefit of a 200-mile limit, one of which being Iceland, and with a flash of inspiration he 'enlightened' me by shouting back "ah, but don't you realise that Iceland is one hundred percent dependent on fishing?" - this with a satisfied smirk on his face. I said "you have fisherman here today from all over Britain who are as equally dependent on fishing as those from Iceland, Norway and all the rest of the world, but you are inferring that we are inferior to them". On the way out of that meeting, basically a wasted afternoon, I refused to shake hands with the Secretary of State and Lord Mansfield - as I told them, the reason being that all they had given me was evasive answers. For me to have expected anything other from politicians I must have been a perfect example of an innocent in Paris. Whilst all the rest of the world hold their fishermen in high regard and consider them a valuable asset, sadly British fishermen are regarded as expendable pawns in the game of politics.

Fishing boats require to have an annual refit and painting, usually done at the various shipyards around Britain, and as my first two boats *Guiding Star* and *Maureen* both had Gardner engines, the engine overhaul was done with John and Henry Fleetwood in Lossiemouth who specialised in Gardner engines. The rest of the repairs, including the painting, were taken care of by Jones' shipyard there. On one of these occasions we were told to moor inside two other boats also undergoing their annual refit, and then I started going through the list of repairs with Jackie the foreman in charge of the slip. First on the agenda was to renew the dry exhaust from the engine up through the galley deck to the roof. It had to be cut out with the burning gear, which job the shipyard men had begun working on whilst I was going through the rest of the work with Jackie. I told my crew that I would join them shortly at the bus stop as our discussion regarding repairs was just about over. No sooner had I left the boat than I was stopped by a Board of Trade official who had been told that I was the skipper of the *Maureen*, who said "you do not have a wireless operator's licence", which was the first time I had heard of this requirement. I said "that's no problem, I've had plenty of experience and fully understand all the requirements. Also I'm on my way to catch the bus home". He replied "have it your way, but unless you complete this test to my satisfaction your boat cannot go to sea, full stop". Faced with this ultimatum I called to my crew that I would miss the bus but would be home later. We then both proceeded to the cabin of the *Maureen* where he produced the necessary form, saying to me "it's vital that you understand all the correct procedures needed for any emergency", when the engine room door flew open and two workmen leapt out shouting "she's on fire under the fuel tank". The fuel tanks on either side were sheathed with wood panelling on the inside, and what had happened was that a piece of molten metal from the burning going on overhead had dropped down between the panelling and the fuel tank. All was a mass of flames so we rushed up on deck. The foreman was shouting to his men "cast off the two boats tied to the *Maureen* - if she goes up she will take them with her. Also, phone for the Elgin fire brigade immediately". The fact that I switched on the smothering gas cylinders, a switch which also activates a screaming siren, needed a few minutes to explain to Jackie - "hang on, forget the fire brigade, this cuts off the oxygen and with the galley door shut should put out the fire very soon". Which it did. Earlier there had been the option of installing either a sprinkler system in the engine room or the smothering gas - this incident proved to me how effective the gas one was. The Board of Trade official, who had now returned back on board the boat, said "just sign this certificate - I'm satisfied that you know what to do in an emergency". My boat was insured by the Buckie insurance company who had an office above the harbour in Lossiemouth, and Dennis the manager appeared on the scene saying "it's a good job, Donald, that you were still there to switch on the smothering gas, thus possibly saving the boat". I said "on the contrary, Dennis, I'm now realising that it could be one of my biggest blunders". He said "I'm not following you, Donald". I explained that had I not been kept behind with the B.O.T. official there was every chance that the boat could have ended up a write-off through no fault of mine, and being fully insured it would have enabled me to go ahead for a higher-powered boat. My reasoning was entirely opposite to Dennis', whose opinion of course was one of what it could have cost their insurance company, and then when I suggested a small remuneration to me from his company for my part in saving the boat it fell on deaf ears.

Another incident that happened when I was prawn trawling at the Skate Hole about 80 miles north east of Buckie was that whilst hauling the trawl, the footrope with rubbers and chain fouled the prop - a very common occurrence, usually cleared by strapping up the footrope on both quarters and thrashing it out with the prop. This time however, after blasting it clear by this method, the bosom chain, about three fathoms long of half-inch chain which had been tied along the footrope, was now wrapped around the propeller and when I began to steam, the loose end of the chain was flaying against the hull above the prop which I realised could cut through the skin and also wreck both the stern post and the propeller. My first thought was to contact one of the boats in the area to tow me ashore, but as it was only Tuesday and all were enjoying good fishing I decided to go overboard and attempt to unwind the chain. Tying a rope around my waist I went over and after repeatedly diving and surfacing in a force 5 breeze with the *Maureen* wallowing about, I finally unwound the chain and the crew hauled me back on board with the power block. That Friday, after landing in Buckie, I told the representative of the Buckie insurance company how, by going over the side and clearing the chain from the propeller myself, I had saved them the cost of my being towed ashore. But once again no cash was forthcoming. The fact that I had wrecked the *Guiding Star* the previous year, which had also been insured through them, doubtless contributed largely to the fact that D. Patience did not seem to be exactly regarded as their blue-eyed boy and was not in line for ex-gratia handouts.

The Tiree passage was an area that all prawn boats fishing the South Minch knew well, as whenever the fishing in the South Minch eased off you were certain of catching bulk prawns there, mostly small ones, but the quantity compensated for the poor quality. One Saturday when I was fishing with the *Maureen* along with a personal friend of mine, Angus, the skipper of the Stornoway boat the *Girl Norma*, we both tied up for the night at the small stone pier at Bunessan in Mull, as you only caught the prawns during daylight hours. Both crews made their way up to the local hotel about half a mile from the pier. After an enjoyable few hours with both crews, the locals and the Constable, by closing time it had turned into a miserable night with a strong wind and rain, so the Constable told us that rather than our all getting soaked his wife would drive us down to our boats - an offer gratefully accepted.

Dad and myself during summer holidays in the cabin of the Maureen in Bunsen Harbour, Isle of Mull

Angus and I were the first to arrive at the pier; we were in the back seat of the car and between us was a brown carrier bag which I presumed belonged to Angus, and took to my boat where we had decided to continue with the ceilidh for both crews.

I found that the bag contained two bottles of King George V whisky and although it was only mugs, no glasses, we were having an extended enjoyable evening with a mixture of Gaelic and Auchie traditional folk songs, until some time later a furious Constable arrived in my cabin shouting "out, you lousy bastards - after my wife running you down to your boats you even stole my going-away present". Apparently the two bottles were his present from the community earlier that evening as he was leaving Banessan that weekend for a different posting. The mistake

Dad and myself working the winch –
prawn fishing 1971 aboard the Maureen
(not the same Health & Safety Rules in 'them days')

was obviously an innocent one as I had presumed Angus had bought the bottles and he thought I had, but on reflection it would have been a rather extravagant carry-out for prawn fishermen. At that time a few cans of beer would have been the norm. But this explanation in no way placated the furious Constable. When Angus advised him to calm down and have a dram of the whisky, this was the final insult - he grabbed the remains of the two bottles and swore that never again would he go out of his way to help so-and-so fishermen. It was a genuine case of mistaken identity unanimously accepted by both crews and today would have been cleared no problem by the court of human rights in Brussels.

My obsession with fishing gear was given a final boost when I found out that the net manufacturers in Scotland, W J Knox and Stuart Jack, were selling off their surplus gear, including cancelled orders world wide, which was published in a catalogue sent to their customers. I would spend many hours scrutinising these lists, always ending up deciding that I would be able to make use of the surplus gear. The fact that all this clearance stock was being sold off at a fraction of its true cost was an added incentive for me. I could always convince myself that at some time in the future I would be able to use the gear. To say that this obsession was getting out of hand would be to put it mildly and things eventually came to a head when one day a lorry-load of bales of netting and miles of nylon line hanks arrived at our home in the village and Maureen, now driven to distraction, finally decided that enough was enough. I was given the ultimatum that for the foreseeable future this maniacal obsession with stockpiling surplus gear had to stop, for when I arrived home one weekend even our bedroom was piled up with boxes and bales of sheeting. Maureen stated in no uncertain terms that I had much more important priorities - essentials that had to come first.

One bargain that I purchased was a mountain of 7½ inch

cod net sheets, which was a cancelled order originally destined for Canada and which I decided to rig out for the West Coast cod fishing. We began rigging out in the village hall with all the crew involved. This was in the early sixties before leadline footropes were invented and to sink the nets to the sea bed the method at that time consisted of making sandbags from hessian netting about eighteen inches long and two inches in diameter to tie along the footrope every few fathoms. I obtained a bale of grain sacks from a warehouse in Inverness and with another flash of inspiration decided what better place to have them sewn up than Porterfield Prison in Inverness where I had an interview with the Superintendent who told me he would give me a price for making them in a few days' time - a total of three thousand yards sewn up. On receiving a quote of fifty pounds from Porterfield I decided to ask my Uncle Jim, who had served his time as a sailmaker, if he would make them for me as I had two heavy duty sewing machines. To which he said "no trouble, Donald" and after showing me how to work one of them we began production. In a very short time, during which Jim had done ninety per cent of the sewing, they were made. The headline floats were at that time the same glass balls as we used for deep water line fishing. We ended up rigging about sixty nets and set off for the cod fishing at Gairloch where the local boats were having heavy fishing - only for me to realise to my dismay that once again I had, through lack of patience and forethought, made a colossal blunder. Cod fishing in the West Coast consisted mainly of sprag-sized cod and the ideal mesh size was 6 to 6½ inches. We spent two weeks fruitlessly shooting our gear alongside that of the local boats through dense marks of cod, but where they were filling their boats to the hatches, the cod were swimming clean through our 7½ inch mesh. After two weeks of this fiasco the crew had had enough and packed it in and I was left with only one crew member, Peter Hansell from Whitby. We tied up the boat in Ullapool for the weekend, then decided to take on board the prawn trawl gear and attempt to work the *Maureen* two-handed.

When we arrived in Ullapool on the Sunday afternoon with a lorry with the trawl gear to unload, we had to unload the cod nets first and I needed at least one other person for this, so approached the skipper of the pleasure boat, the *Blaven*, Alistair Muil, and asked if he would give us a hand to take the gear ashore. To which he readily consented and as it was the off season for him he also agreed to join us as one of the crew. Our first tow on Monday was in the deep water from the Rhu Rea light north for about sixty boxes of dogfish, and we ended up with over two hundred for the day. As the price in Lochinver was only about fifteen shillings per box we decided to consign them to Grimsby, which normally was the best market for them in Britain. Unfortunately, when they arrived in Grimsby it was awash with dogs and after transport and other expenses were deducted it turned out to be another blunder as we only cleared about £28. Deciding that the prawns would be a better bet we went over to the Stornoway side to concentrate on prawn fishing and on the first tow on Tuesday we had a double lift of small prawns - as Alistair said, "thank God for that big haul". I decided that as this was Alistair's first time at the fishing Peter and I would have to tail the prawns, and after I had explained the rudiments of the Decca to Alistair he would then take over the skipper's job in the wheelhouse. No sooner would we have the deck clear when it was 'heave up' again - it was non-stop work. So when preparing our grub I had a large broth pan on the stove and would keep lobbing in anything from tins of beans, corned beef, a handful of prawn tails, fillets of fish and a large squid tail which would surface every time the ladle was used. This was our basic staple diet for the trip, breakfast, dinner and supper and to vary the menu I had no shortage of raw and tinned ingredients to top up the pot.

From the fifties to the early sixties it was still possible to make a living at the lines. One of the last times I tried line fishing was after I had wrecked the *Guiding Star* and had decided to give it a go in the *Maureen* after the winter herring fishing. My first shot was in the loch at Ullapool - as I had a different crew I had decided to shoot in the sheltered waters to see if it worked. We had about two and a half tons of skate that haul, and as I now knew it was pointless shooting there again as skate are wiped out in one go, I decided to try some of my old shots in the Minch, North and South. I also knew that any area that had been prawn-trawled for any length of time was a total waste of time trying. For line fishing I had to concentrate on some place that was not suffering the effects of trawl.

One area that was virtually virgin ground was the north side of the Stoer Bank, where we shot the lines in two fleets from the shore out. This was one of the best hauls I ever had, a mixture of skate, cod and nine halibut of from four to nine stone. The next day's fishing was down to about a quarter of that, so we landed in Ullapool, took on board six crans of bait, and as I had tried most of the other places with little to show for it I decided to make for west of Shetland. We shot the lines north of Foula, on the edge from eighty to one hundred fathoms, and hauled next day with a dogfish on every hook but as it so happened there was no demand for them. When I told the crew that we may as well have a few shots at the Faroe Bank they flatly refused and as I was faced with a nine to one situation and Foula to me was less attractive than Pitcairn Island, I decided to call it a day. We headed for Fraserburgh, dumped the fleet ashore and told the salesman to give them away free.

When trawling once with the *Maureen* in the South Minch, I was having a problem with my trawl gear and we were only catching about half the amount of fish and prawns that the other boats towing in the area were catching. Every haul I would alter something - on the trawl-doors, or sweeps, spreaders - with an increasingly disillusioned crew, until when trawling up one tow, even before the trawl doors were alongside the trawl burst onto the surface about two hundred yards astern - a bulging mass. The crew were shouting "you've done it this time, Donald". Doing my best not to appear excited I said "yes, it's that extra chain I put on the lower wing end that's solved the problem". My sense of achievement was short-lived when, instead of a massive haul of fish, we found a badly-decomposed whale about forty-five feet long stuck in the funnel of the trawl. We had on board a long pole with a scythe blade attached to it for cutting out net from the propellers, and now with the carcase alongside, belly up, we had to cut it out of the net. Whenever we sliced into it the smell of escaping rotten gas was so bad that we could each only stand it for a few minutes at a time until after about an hour we had finally cut it clear. Back to the drawing board once again, with a very deflated skipper having at least learnt one lesson, which was to beware of getting exultant too soon.

Deep ocean troughs have always had a fascination for me as when line fishing these were where the best fish congregated - hake, skate, cod, monkfish etc - and once when I had to clear out from Barra Head waters with a southerly gale I decided to have a go at fishing the deepest waters of the trink. This was a long trough with three deep holes in the middle, as deep as one hundred and sixty fathoms, considered to contain boulders; consequently the boats fish the edges from sixty to eighty fathoms and keep clear of the deepest holes. We shot the trawl on the edge of the first hole in eighty fathoms and slackened out more warp as we deepened to the middle of the hole. We were forced to heave up after thirty minutes as we became stuck leaving the hole. No damage, or boulders, but an excellent haul for the short tow. Forty boxes, half roker skate, half monkfish and a few large hake. Concentrating on these holes only we landed on Wednesday in Mallaig with two hundred and forty boxes of the same quality, roughly half monkfish and half roker skate, plus a few boxes of large hake. After landing the catch we headed straight back out and landed another two hundred boxes on Friday, again no boulders.

This was a one-off chance from the trink for me as afterwards it was well watched by other boats. Other deep water troughs that provided excellent fishing in those days for both fish and prawns were on both sides of Raasay Island, which before the introduction of the prawn trawl was only fished with lines or nets for hake, cod and dogfish. The three-mile limit was in force in those days, which created a cat and mouse situation as it was very tempting to tow in those sheltered waters, sounds and lochs as they were where you caught the best quality fish and prawns. This type of fishing was ideal for me as it provided a thrill lacking in the open waters of the Minches; inevitably resulting in many escapades with the fishery cruisers and creating a gamble of wits on both sides. One tactic used later by the fishery cruisers, which resulted in many boats being caught and was considered by the prawners as "not quite cricket", was for the cruiser to steam out into the Minch whilst leaving the high speed inflatable out of sight behind a small island, then when the unwary trawlers considered it now safe to tow 'inside' they got caught by the inflatable's popping out. Through the grapevine and with some unofficial help from those who could tune into the fisheries cruisers' WT band, the prawn fleet were able to pretty well keep tabs on all those fishery cruisers.

Whilst dodging along with a fleet of trawlers outside the three-mile line off Trodday island, where the fishing was so poor that it was a waste of time shooting the gear, but also being aware that the *Minna*, the cruiser, was in Portree, I decided to take a gamble and tow up Portree Sound close in to the Raasay side. My theory was that as the captain of the cruiser knew full well that his whereabouts were common knowledge on all the boats, he would think that none would be so stupid as to venture 'inside'. We shot away abreast Rona light and were towing in towards Rona Sound in the deep water on a flat calm summer's day, when after an hour's towing the *Minna* emerged out of Portree steaming north slowly along the Skye shore towards the Minch. I told my crew to keep out of sight and slowed the *Maureen* down until we were just edging through the water and, as the boat was painted green, hoping it would blend in with the foliage on the shore-side. This was one of the longest hours of my poaching life, as we could see every movement on board the *Minna* as she steamed slowly out into the Minch. Despite the fact that we had had a good haul and an excellent day's fishing, I decided against pushing my luck in that manner again.

One of the best alibis that any fishing cruiser must have heard was on the occasion when a Fraserburgh prawn boat, the *Aurora*, who definitely topped my record for poaching, decided on seeing the cruiser to slip his trawl doors fastened to a few prawn pots with a rope to a buoy, then steamed away from them. When boarded by the cruiser, with his deck full of prawns, warps on his drums, trawl on his quarter but no trawl doors, he was accused of illegal fishing. The law was that it was in fact legal to catch prawns with a net if no doors were used, so the skipper told the boarding party that he was catching prawns without using doors and also said "I'll tell you something else, we are doing OK as well". Some you win, some you lose. This was an accepted fact by all concerned but the introduction of the spotter plane using camera evidence was fast closing the door for legitimate poachers like myself.

The crunch came for me when I was trawling at the east side of Raasay island with my partner, Sandy Patience, of the *Argosy*. The weather was a north-west gale at the time and as we were hauling up a Buckie boat, the *Seafarer,* called me up as he was fouled up with his net in the propeller three miles north of Rona, asking me to tow him to

Gairloch. I assured the skipper that I would be under way in a short time after getting my gear on board, but when we were hauling the net the spotter plane swooped over Raasay, circled my boat twice, and also the *Argosy,* then repeated the performance when the cod end was spilling the haul on deck. This was the first time I had been caught by this foul method, which entailed some devious thinking as we steamed up to and consequently towed the *Seafarer* to Gairloch. On arrival there I immediately phoned the Fisheries department in Edinburgh to whom I explained the situation my way. I told them that whilst steaming for Mallaig with a north-west gale I had been contacted by the *Seafarer*, fouled up, requesting me to tow him to Gairloch. And as I had only a hundred and fourteen HP engine, in those weather conditions I decided to clear my quarter of the two trawls by gilsoning them amidship to enable me to use a towing bridle. But as we were in the process of heaving the second trawl amidship the spotter plane circled overhead, obviously thinking that we were fishing illegally. The Edinburgh office reassured me that they understood the situation, accepting my explanation. Six months later I was amazed to receive a summons for illegal fishing from the Sheriff in Portree concerning that incident, which I understood had been cleared up previously by my telephone call to the Edinburgh office. I immediately telephoned the Sheriff in Portree stating this fact and advising him to scrub the charge as I had already been cleared by the Edinburgh office, and I would have a box of kippers sent to him from Mallaig for his trouble. He replied "the kippers will be very acceptable, but I can tell you something, Mr. Patience, that you don't know. When the aerial photographs were developed they showed in detail a large bag of fish and prawns emptying onto your deck, which you cannot catch by gilsoning empty trawls amidship". The Mallaig kippers as always must have been top quality as we were only fined £50 each.

One Sunday when we were stormbound in Mallaig I was walking along the quay about 10 am - it was blowing a gale - when I met a couple of cyclists who asked me if the Skye ferry would be running. I in turn asked a friend of mine, Peter Downie, who was also out for a morning stroll, and he told me that the summer Sunday service would not begin until next month. I told the couple this, adding that were it not for the fact that my boat was the inside one of a tier of six on account of the weather conditions, I could easily have given them a run across to pass the time. However, if they were interested they would be very welcome to join me and my crew for dinner at one o'clock, as it would be Monday before they could cross on the steamer to Skye - to which they readily agreed. When I told Roddy, who was busy preparing the dinner, that a couple of American cyclists stranded in Mallaig would be joining us for the meal, he said "that's no problem but hang on until I check the cutlery. I think some was chucked overboard by mistake last week. Yes, we are short of a knife and two forks". So I said I would get some from Ewan, the manager of the Marine Hotel, when he opened. I explained this to Ewan saying I had felt sorry for them and Ewan said it was no trouble at all and handed me the cutlery, adding "they are also booked in here for full board". They were obviously not on as tight a budget as I had at first presumed. What I had noticed was that their bicycles were completely different from the usual ones.

Anyway, at dinnertime they arrived at the *Maureen* and the husband handed down a hamper containing bottles of wine, saying it was always the custom back home to provide the wine when invited out for a meal. All new protocol to me. After we had all been introduced on first-name terms, Roddy, who was an excellent cook, excelled himself - the meal, roast beef with yorkshire pudding and all the trimmings and ending with a fantastic trifle, was thoroughly enjoyed by all, and complemented by the wine so kindly provided. When I brought up the subject of their bicycles being very different from most, Milton explained that he was an inventor and had made them himself from high-tensile aircraft alloy - the only parts he had not made were the tyres and tubes - and added that each was insured for $3000. He then enlightened me as to the reason why both he and his wife were using this means of transport, saying "we are millionaires, I am president of the Hexseal Company, Brooklyn, New York - we have a luxury yacht fitted with the *Loran*, and every navigational aid for this type of boat, but we arrived at a stage where we were both becoming bored with our lifestyle". I then mentioned that the previous week I had had the Decca navigator installed but still had not got the hang of it. Milton said "produce the manual", and together with his wife, he and I went into the wheelhouse, where between them they went into detailed explanations delivered in a basic, straightforward manner, solving my problems. Milton then explained that they had decided to spend a year of their lives cycling around various parts of the world, having covered so far most of Europe and now Britain, ending up with Scotland, saying it had been a fantastic experience. They said that so far ours was the best hospitality they had encountered in their travels - adding that Roddy's trifle was 'out of this world'. By this time, and whilst we consumed the wine, they had been told many of my past experiences - wrecking the *Guiding Star*, purchasing the *Accumulator*, now named *Maureen* after my wife and which we were all then on board. Milton then asked what our average earnings were for this type of boat in Scotland and I replied that it could fluctuate from four to ten thousand a year for the top-boat. He said "I can tell you for a fact, as we have fishermen friends at home, that in the USA you could triple your earnings. We ourselves have no family, but talk the matter over with your wife and if you are both interested in emigrating to America to fish there I will provide you with a modern fishing vessel. It would also be a point of interest to us both". He then handed me his engraved card "Milton Morse, President of the Hexseal Company, Brooklyn, New York".

But after discussing the matter with Maureen and the family we decided that we were quite happy with our lifestyle in Scotland. However, it did all emphasise to me how wrong one can be with first impressions and how a small act of kindness could change one's lifestyle - a gesture such as meeting and inviting a couple of strangers on board for a meal and have it turn into a highlight that will always be remembered. It did a lot to compensate for the all-too-often daily grind of fishing, as did meeting new people in all the different ports - always an enhancing experience, whether they be other fishermen or folk on holiday.

Another encounter which took place in Mallaig happened when we were tied up there on one occasion with a gear-box problem which needed a few days' work on it. An ex-Stornoway boat, the *Strenuous,* arrived in, also with an engine problem, and tied up alongside the *Maureen*. Its skipper and two of a crew were transporting the boat to Portsmouth as it had been sold to there. When I spoke to them and found out that they would also be tied up here for a few days I suggested that as I had the bigger boat they were welcome to have their meals with us - an invitation they accepted with pleasure. The skipper of the *Strenuous* was a Latvian captain, named George Savage, who was having a 90-ft. M.M.S. (motor minesweeper) converted to a fishing trawler with refrigeration etc. He was one of the most interesting men I ever had the pleasure of encountering. Pre-war his family had had a shipping company in Riga, and when Latvia was occupied by the Germans he was given the option of either becoming a prisoner of war or serving in the German Navy - which later he did, as an officer. However, at the end of the war in '45, when his country was by then occupied by the Russians, he was in a situation where because of his having served in the German Navy there was every chance of his ending in a prisoner of war camp, or worse. So he and his family rowed across the Baltic Sea to Sweden. They then made their way to Britain where, after getting the family established and with the qualifications he had, he became captain of an oil tanker - he and his family were then living at Golders Green in London.

He had been on a regular run delivering oil from the Persian Gulf to West Africa, mostly to Dakar, when he was approached one day by a Chinese gentleman who asked him if he would be interested in becoming captain of a fishing side-trawler in their Company at more than double his existing salary, which would be paid into a Swiss bank every month. George said straight away that he had no experience of fishing, but was assured that this was no problem as the African mate would handle the fishing and he would only be required to captain the vessel. On that basis George decided it was an attractive proposition, and on his first trip he saw that the mate, who was well over six feet tall with a very powerful physique, was totally competent fishing-wise and also had the full respect of the crew. One day, whilst they were hauling in the trawl on the starboard side, which entailed the crew's dragging it in manually over the gunwale up to the cod end, a few large sharks arrived on the scene, attracted by the fish. The trawler was rolling up to the gunwale with the heavy swell and one of the crew panicked and rushed farther inboard, shouting to the mate about the sharks. The mate picked up the deck hand and threw him straight at the sharks. George, witnessing this from the bridge, thought "this is murder". However, as he was told by the mate later, the splash would have scared off the sharks temporarily and when the man hit the water his arms and legs were windmilling so fast that he was back on board in a matter of seconds. Needless to say, no-one left his place again whilst hauling the trawl. The area where they were fishing was a few miles off the Gold Coast and he had been told it extended for hundreds of miles - every few hours they

133

would heave up with a good mixed bag of fish containing at least half a ton of jumbo prawns, which George was surprised to see were all thrown back as, he was told, there was no demand for them. The fact that the trawler was not fitted with refrigeration, carrying only ice, was a great disadvantage and they had to land every few days.

After two years of this lucrative employment he had decided to launch out and get his own vessel, the M.M.S. now being converted in Portsmouth, and planned to keep the prawns as well and consign them in a freezer container to either Britain, France or Spain, which would double the value of the catch. As he explained to me, "that area is wide open for anyone with experience and his own vessel to make a lot of money in just a few years". He then offered "once I get back fishing in Africa in a few months' time, and with another few months to get established, if things work out as planned I'll get in touch with you, pay for the cost of refrigeration and the copper sheathing which is a must for a wooden vessel, and we could fish together there". I was very interested in this generous offer, but the following year I received a short letter from him stating that the situation had completely changed - that part of Africa had declared independence, the inhabitants now had complete control of their own country and all foreign fishing vessels were excluded.

As already mentioned, I have always been fascinated by deep water troughs - right from the time when we first became involved in great line fishing, which was a relatively efficient method of finding the best depths at which the different species congregated. The West Coast and the North Sea were both alive with fish in post-war years and the biggest problem facing all fishermen at the time was the control price for fish. The guaranteed price for herring, which had held all through those years and for a few years after, was abolished. It threw the industry into total chaos. This was when every boat yard in Britain was fully employed expanding the fishing fleets. One boat yard in particular, James Noble in Fraserburgh, was launching one ring net boat a month (some of which are still fishing up to the present day).

All too often the markets were unable to cope with the ever-increasing landings - curers that salted the herring, canning factories for human consumption, dog food, fish meal factories for meal and oil, were hardly making a dent in the massive shoals. I remember one summer in Fraserburgh when the fish meal factory ran out of space to stow the surplus herring in its buildings - whilst awaiting a clearance the fish were left outside in open forty-gallon drums sprayed with a solution to prevent them from rotting. Whatever it was they were sprayed with caused the seagulls, which had been enjoying an unlimited free supply of their traditional herring menu, to lose all their feathers. The sight of bald seagulls walking on the streets immediately put an end to this practice and all drums were covered thereafter.

One of the most shameful practices ever to be brought in by the last Government was the way it enforced decommissioning to be applied to cut back the fishing fleet – 'slash and burn'. All that should have been needed was for the fishermen to give up their licences and then at least allow those craftmanship-built vessels to be sold for conversion to pleasure boats or some other such use. But no, the powers-that-be stipulated that every trace of those boats had to vanish, even going so far as to deny their being kept for maritime museums. Many of those boats were still in perfect condition and it must have been heartbreaking for the craftsmen that built them and the fishermen that sailed them to witness this senseless and sadistic policy. An old picture I have never forgotten was of a derelict sailing herring boat lying on its beam ends on a mud flat, showing the quarter with the steering wheel silhouetted against a setting sun and the words "Oh for the touch of a loving hand and the sound of a voice that is gone".

Future generations will look back aghast at the politicians who were happy to spend over half a million pounds in lifting the rotten frames of the *Mary Rose* from the Thames whilst at the same time denying the preservation of the finest wooden fishing vessels, mostly built in Scotland, and their place in history. I could fill a complete book with the names of the boat builders from the Borders, East and West, not forgetting England and Ireland, which all took pride in their individual construction of the state-of-the-art boats, an art that is gone forever. The sound of the adze and caulking hammers will never again resound in boat yards around Britain. Possibly one or two will be kept as a tourist feature, but it is a disgrace for a once top-line maritime nation. Britain, who only half a century ago was one of the top maritime nations in the world, has now been relegated to third world status. Edward Heath will go down in history as the one who put the final nail in the coffin of the United Kingdom fishing industry - an action ever since condoned by subsequent Governments. Those involved in the drift net herring fishing after the war will always remember the days when nightfall approached and the herring rose to the surface, and the man on watch called to the crew "they are starting to play". At first just a few plops, but at times the whole sea would become a boiling mass, with a sound like a torrential monsoon as millions of herring leapt in a frenzy. This pattern of behaviour is seldom seen nowadays as modern hi-tech methods drive the shoals ever deeper.

When trawling with my partner Sandy both vessels were rigged out with identical pair trawls made by Boris of Fleetwood, eighteen fathom box trawls starting at the mouth with 6" to the 2" mesh herring bag - this was when the pair trawl was in its infancy and the shoals were still very prolific. Our first tow was in Loch Ouirn (Odhairn), about twelve miles south of Stornoway, where we detected a heavy shoal of herring. The weather conditions were a north

136

easterly gale as we steamed the trawl at the head of the loch and commenced towing out through the heavy mark and we decided to heave up at the sea side of the loch. By this time we were encountering heavy seas away from the shelter of the loch. When we attempted to come alongside to haul the trawl, both vessels were almost standing on end and owing to the fact that the *Maureen* was a bigger boat we were smashing each other up. I shouted out "let go another fifty fathoms spread out, we must turn around and tow back into the sheltered waters at the head of the loch to haul the net" - which we did.

In the winter time the herring were always inclined to seek the rock face and the method of catching them with the pair trawl, as proved by all vessels involved in this method of fishing, was as follows - irrespective of the weather conditions, gales and all. Shoot the trawl in the shelter of a loch, tow out and the inside vessel would be, as we classed it, rock bouncing, and at the same time flashing its searchlight to scare the herring off the cliff face onto the mouth of the trawl, then heave up in the next loch in sheltered water where the partner boat held you in tow until the catch was bagged on board. This method of fishing was not for the faint-hearted as all too often the inside boat was literally scraping the barnacles off the cliffs amongst exploding heavy seas. My partner would insist on saying to me when I was the inside boat "go further in, Donald". I said "Sandy, if I go any further in I will need caterpillar tracks on the *Maureen*". To say that my partner was a desperado was to put it mildly, but he was the partner that I needed at that time as in some ways I had been trying to turn the clock back with static methods of fishing lines, drift nets etc.

As the herring shoals were becoming depleted, to move with the times it was obvious that bigger boats with more horse power were essential. To quote just one example: I shot my trawl to tow though a white line mark off Loch

Shell - this is the heaviest concentration of herring that the echo sounder can show - and we were followed by a Fraserburgh pair who towed behind us. The first pair to tow the mark, which was us, should have the best haul - I heaved up for a total of two tons. The Fraserburgh boats behind us had twelve tons. Sandy said "there must be something wrong with your net". I said "Sandy, the difference is that we have straw in our stables, they have horses". 114hp as compared with 400hp - as King Richard said a long time ago *"A horse, a horse, my Kingdom for a horse"*. We both realised that to be competitive we would have to move with the times. My partner ordered a new boat, the *Adventurer*,

Adventurer INS 8 - Skipper Sandy Patience
A poor day off Barra Head - 1980

whilst I was dithering with my old vessel, and at the last moment I bought a second-hand boat, the *Ocean Trust*, with a 350hp Kelvin engine. This was a rushed decision and I very soon realised that I was landed with a pig in a poke, as of my two years with this boat half that time was spent in dock, which cost a fortune in repairs and lost fishing time. Another example of what my father said about patience - the virtue that I lacked was once again costing me dearly.

We were prawn trawling at Shields in '68 with the *Maureen* and a large fleet of other prawners, fishing the Farne and Dunstable deeps and tied up for the weekend at North Shields on the Saturday when the salesman informed me that our own salesman at home had contacted him with a message for me. "Advise come home Kessock herring fishing started yesterday". In those days, as soon as the Kessock fishing began a similar urge to that experienced by migratory flocks affected all Avoch fishermen. One example being when an old fisherman on his deathbed was visited by a friend who asked him "how are you feeling today Dan?", he replied "how do you expect me to be feeling when every Avoch boat is tied up at Inverness full to the hatches?". Despite the fact that it was blowing a NE gale I decided to leave immediately and my uncle Will commented to both Hugh and Ian "this will be a toasty grill trip" - insinuating that no food would be cooked in those conditions. Seven hours later, about 2am on the Sunday morning, we were making heavy weather as it was now about force 10 NE, when Will came into the wheelhouse saying "there's a lot of water in the engine room and the engine bilge pump cannot cope, we will need to use the two deck pumps too". Slowing the boat down I told Will to keep dodging head to wind and when we all went out on deck we saw that the spare trawl on the port deck amidships was gone with only the wing end tied to the stringer left trailing over the side. It had been cut by the prop when the trawl went overboard. As it was rigged with nylon rope and grass rope it had cut easily. Had it been rigged with combination wire and rubbers the prop might well have been severely damaged and the consequences of this disastrous. It was Monday morning before we finally arrived home, taking almost twice as long as normal, and the elusive Kessocks had vanished as well.

My partner Sandy, with the *Adventurer*, and I became involved in the Isle of Man herring fishing in '72. Sandy, who had had the foresight to build a modern fishing vessel, was ideally placed to fish with our other two partner vessels the *Mystic* and the *Wisteria*, identical new boats to the *Adventurer*, whilst I had bought an 18-year-old boat, the *Ocean Trust*, without even having the basic savvy to have it surveyed. I had been strongly advised by my salesman Hugh Patience, M.D.M. Buckie, not to purchase the boat - as he said, "we do not want to be involved". As usual, any advice to me fell on deaf ears, which I found out the hard way. This was the time when herring prices were at their peak, up to £40 per unit of 100 kilos, and landings were restricted which kept the price high. One day in particular, when landing at the breakwater quay at Douglas, we had a few units surplus to our quota and it was usual practice to give these free to anyone interested. Just at that time there was a police van above the boat with a sergeant and constable, so I asked them if they could use some of the surplus herring for the rest of the police force. I went up to the police headquarters in the van with six boxes of herring and the Superintendent asked me why I was giving them for nothing - "what is the catch?" I said there was no catch, "but memorise my features, possibly sometime I will require your help". This relationship stood us in good terms over the years, when we enjoyed some of the best season's fishing with some of those very friendly islanders - something which all Scottish fishermen remember with nostalgia.

One morning while prawn trawling out in Loch Scridan along the cliff face at Bunessan on a flat calm sunny day I was relieved for breakfast by one of the crew and was just finishing it when the *Maureen* began pitching about. From a flat calm we were now facing a freak severe gale on the broadside and were in imminent danger of piling up on the rocks which were now only about fifty yards away, and Roddy said "I can't get her to steer". We were either mudding up or had picked up a heavy object. Shouting to the crew to slack out fifty fathoms of warp to get the boat head to wind, I was able to tow the gear to a safe distance offshore and after about half an hour the wind had dropped again, enabling us to haul the gear. With the net heaved up to the quarter, when hauling up the bag it was obvious that what I had first thought, that the net had mudded up, was not the case as underneath a good haul of prawns, with a cloud of rusty water, we had picked up a mine. A short time previously my partner skipper, Sandy, with his first boat the *Argosy,* had also picked up a mine in this area and had followed the correct procedure of towing it into shallow water, slackening away the trawl and marking it with a buoy, then contacting the mine disposal squad at Rosyth to come and render it safe. After which he was able to retrieve his trawl and hoped he would be paid compensation. He was, however, told that compensation was only paid for a certain type of mine and was not applicable to this one. The fact that I was working on a very tight budget and this was virtually a new trawl with a good haul of prawns on top of the mine, and with every possibility of receiving the same treatment as my partner and not be eligible for compensation, I decided to do it my way. I slackened away the trawl with a few fathoms of warp and towed it into sheltered water where I once again heaved the bag alongside at the starboard gilson derrick and put a running bowline around the cod end between the mine and the prawns. Then with one of the crew keeping the tension on this rope I lay over the side to cut the cod end rope and jettison the mine, and one of the crew said "this is pure madness, the net seems more important than our lives", to which I replied "anyone who is concerned about his safety go over to the port side". The fact that we were able to save the bag of prawns and continue fishing does not in any way mean that I made the correct decision but only emphasises that in every case where a mine, bomb or whatever is picked up, adequate compensation should be the Government's priority for fishing vessels. Had any of the horns been intact on the mine I would never have done what I did as I had been told at a lecture on mines in the National Service 'a mine is never safe, even a change in temperature from the sea to air can set it off, and if you ever end up with one on deck keep the hose on it'. The instructor had also told us that, even after seventy years, the first mines ever laid in the Turkish war were still active when lifted.

I shall never forget one day in '68, steaming from Mallaig to Barra Head in December, when one of my crew observed a pod of three whales blowing. It was the only time in my life that I have witnessed the largest known living animal, the 'rorqual' a genus which includes the blue whale, or 'finback whale'. They reminded me of three submarines, swimming slowly along on the surface and blowing occasionally. My vessel at that time was the *Maureen*, INS 215, sixty-five feet long, and as I cruised slowly beside them we estimated that lengthwise they were from seventy to possibly (the largest) about eighty-five feet. This was between the island of Rhum and Skye - to be more exact the island of Soay. To see those fantastic docile animals, which have been hunted to near extinction, was one of the saddest spectacles I have witnessed in marine life. Going back to the turn of the century when the whaling station was in West Loch Tarbert, one of the largest of this species, over ninety feet long and weighing about one hundred tons, was landed there. The jawbone became the arch for the entrance gate - have we learned anything in the last century? As an old friend of mine, Gilbert Buchan from

Fraserburgh, stated, "there is enough in the sea for man's needs but not for his greed". The oceans are being depleted by modern technology - and I must confess that I am among the culprits - at an alarming rate that nature cannot sustain. The waters around the UK were once one of the most prolific fishing grounds in the world but are being decimated at such a rate that very soon they will be comparable to the Sahara Desert. Have we not learned anything from the collapse of the Newfoundland Banks? One does not require to be a marine biologist to understand that industrial fishing is the death knell of the industry, wiping out the food chain, and the use of the oil to fuel power stations is a crime against humanity.

One of the strictly prohibited areas for fishing was a buoyed area north of Applecross to south of Loch Torridon, about which all the fishermen were informed. Anyone fishing there was liable to a £50,000 fine. You were allowed to steam across it as any devices or cables were on the sea bed. It was involved in experimental work with submarines and torpedo tests. Directly opposite the base there was a heavy herring mark on the echo sounder which we had both noticed a few times previously, always hoping that it would shift either north or south of the prohibited area. The fact that the base had a powerful radar on 24-hour watch and continually called up any boats going north or south warning them to stick to the rules whilst passing was well known, as was the presence of the high speed MOD launch based at Kyle. One particular night when we were having very slack fishing Sandy said "what about having a go at the mark at Applecross? - we will steam in, shoot without deck lights and tow out". I said "okay Sandy but most likely we will be nabbed as they monitor every boat on the radar". The fact that as the mark at night always rises up and at no time would our net be anywhere near the bottom meant that it would be impossible for us to damage any devices on the sea bed would be poor consolation if we were caught. We shot the trawl, towed through the mark and whilst hauling the net the MOD launch arrived on the scene from Kyle and their inflatable came alongside - I was told to come on board to be taken to the launch, where the captain informed me that he had orders to charge us and that we were for the high jump. Knowing full well the severity of the situation and its implications I replied "relax and let's discuss this in a civilised manner - what about a can of beer, possibly Carlsberg Special Brew for me?" By this time we were sitting down in the mess deck. The captain, somewhat taken aback, said "I have orders to escort you both to Kyle to be charged". I said "you know full well if you go ahead with this we are ruined. What about the can of beer?" He replied "unfortunately we only have lager". I said "that's okay". Thankfully it was a civilian crew who manned the MOD launch and as we were now enjoying a diplomatic drink and I assured him that never again would we shoot the net in the proximity of the range the episode was closed. My partner, Sandy, who by this time had finished bagging the catch said to my son, Donald, "I wonder what's keeping your father, he is a long time on board the launch", unaware that I was enjoying a drink at the MOD's expense.

I must emphasise that on the many occasions when I got involved with fisheries cruisers on my poaching episodes over the years, whenever possible they always gave me the benefit of the doubt and behaved like gentlemen, though doing a difficult job. However one must take into consideration the fact that poachers were vital to the fisheries cruisers as without us there would be no need for them. What swung the balance against 'inside fishermen', which sounds better than 'poachers', was the introduction of the spotter plane - as long as we had had only the cruisers to contend with it had been a level playing field as their movements were pretty well monitored with special codes on the WT. This below-the-belt introduction of spotter planes was similar to pitting a becalmed sailing ship against a nuclear submarine, as I found out when both Sandy, who at that time had the *Argosy* and I the *Maureen,* were caught when towing for prawns at the opposite side of Raasay Sound by the spotter plane which photographed us both. You can argue and state your case with a skipper of a cruiser but photographic evidence is conclusive in court.

****

The *Vision*

My fourth vessel was the *Vision*, a 75ft steel vessel with a 500hp engine, built at Bideford in Devon for Bogg Holdings in Bridlington, who sold it to me. I had been involved with my partner Alexander Patience in previous years at the pair trawl for herring, mackerel and sprats on the East and West Coasts, including the Isle of Man, where we fished successfully for most of the year, alternating between white fish and prawns in season.

The Vision OB 390 - Mallaig 1975

Whilst at the white fish west of the Hebrides, mainly for haddock, a record fishing had started up at Rockall where squid had appeared in dense shoals at a time when they were very much in demand for the Spanish market. This was my first venture there and I had been told you only required a six fathom herring bag instead of the white fish 100mm one to catch the squid. On arrival, and after a few tows, I soon found out that to be competitive what was required was a full herring bag about 20 fathoms long to replace the white fish one at the maximum girth to the trawl, as with the short 6 fathom piece most of the squid were simply escaping through the big mesh.

We landed in Mallaig on the Saturday after a few days fishing with 200 boxes of squid and rather than go home for a full length herring bag I bought a secondhand one and set out once again for Rockall where we caught 450 boxes for 2 days. This bonanza lasted for a few weeks where the squid were congregating, mostly in a tow a few miles long from close by the Rock to a submerged reef, 'St. Helen's reef', NE of Rockall. The daylight and darkening hauls were always the best and quite often included large porbeagle sharks feeding off the squid. (One box of squid was £100).

The Vision before being re-registered OB 390

We did land two of these in Lochinver, about 12ft long, but as they only fetched a total of £50 they were a waste of time and afterwards were always jettisoned back into the sea. The last landing that season from the Rock consisted of 450 boxes of haddock at £10 a box, no squid, and we were home for the weekend when Brent Sadler of ITN phoned me from the Kingsmills Hotel in Inverness and asked if I would take him and his team to Rockall to enable them to take photographs of Tom Maclean who had set sail in a yacht from Mallaig - this was to claim Rockall for Britain, with Tom living on it for 40 days. We discussed financial terms and I agreed on a figure of £5000 if I was allowed to fish for two days as well to make it viable. This was agreed on.

We set sail and on arriving at the Rock could discern no signs of life there, so contacted a Fleetwood skipper in the vicinity and asked him if he had seen a yacht in the area during the last few days. We were told no, and after a ship to shore call were informed that the yacht had been forced to abandon the project at Barra Head and that Tom and his team were back in Mallaig. The Fleetwood skipper also informed me that the haddock had vanished too - as he said, "this is the dead period here" - so I decided I had no alternative but to go back to Mallaig with Brent Sadler and his team and then resume normal fishing. But Brent asked me if I would at least shoot the gear and have a tow that they could video, to enable them to salvage something from the fiasco before leaving Rockall. I explained that, as the Fleetwood skipper had said he had had only four boxes from his last tow of four hours, it would be a waste of time but that the following day at Barra Head I would shoot the gear and almost certainly get a good haul of fish which would make an interesting film. This was a tow known as the Pinnacle, where the sea bed rises from 80 fathoms to 40 fathoms like a church steeple and mostly coley are there on one side of it - at that time of little commercial value.

Arriving there with the camera rolling we shot the gear and with Brent in the wheelhouse watching the echo sounder, towed up the south face of the Pinnacle and when going down the other side there they were. A dense shoal heaved up after 30 minutes where the bag burst to the surface like a giant whale. To all those who saw this video on TV it would give the false impression that the sea was alive with fish. However, after bagging them on board we boxed about 100 boxes of the biggest ones and Brent Sadler had action film.

On arrival in Mallaig I intended to resume normal fishing but Brent told me that they were deeply involved with this project in conjunction with Millbury Homes and requested me to hang on whilst they had a discussion. After which he asked me whether we were prepared to land Tom Maclean on the Rock, as on hindsight a yacht would not have been suitable for this purpose. As he said, "the last attempt was a fiasco, through no fault of yours, Donald, but you will be paid in full for it". Plus the fact that by this time we were all good friends and this would provide a welcome break from the normal grind of fishing. So we set sail again for the Rock - this time as well as Brent and his team we had Tom Maclean and *his* team, also a large inflatable on the quarter powered with 2 x 60hp Mercury engines. We arrived once again at the Rock to be faced with a force 6 westerly with the swell rising up the rock more than halfway. This was about 3 o'clock in the afternoon. We launched the inflatable with Tom and his team on board, but he leapt onto the rock at the lower end of the swell and was immediately washed off again by the next sea. Fortunately he had a line attached to him by which he was hauled back to the inflatable and taken back to the *Vision* to recuperate.

Tom was under very high pressure at this time and was determined to land on Rockall, so my son Donald said "I will go in the inflatable this time and make sure that he leaps at the top of the swell", which he did, 'no problem'.

The situation now was that Tom was safely ashore on Rockall but as darkness was then approaching we decided to wait for daylight next morning to land his stores and hut, which he agreed to on his hand radio. Next morning at daybreak, however, when topping up the outboard engines from the jerrycans it was impossible to start them - the plugs kept oiling up, apparently too much lubricating oil in the mixture, and after umpteen attempts Brent said "*you* will have to land the stores, Donald". I said "that is not part of the agreement. Why not put a ship to shore call and have helicopter drop clean petrol in the sea for us to pick up". However we were informed that this was not allowed and there was also the fact that we were outwith the range of the helicopter. I knew that with this sea running it would be suicide to go alongside the rock, but as Tom had a spool of nylon rope and a 40" float I told him to drop the buoy and when it drifted clear of the rock we would pick it up and attach a snatch block to it with an endless rope running through it made from two coils of buoyant polypropylene rope spliced together. When the plastic buoy had drifted a safe distance from the rock, about 50 yards, we picked it up, tied on the snatch block with a large becket to fasten it to the small light on top of the rock and, by means of the endless rope running through it, commenced pulling his stores and hut piecemeal onto the rock. This operation required constant manoeuvring of the *Vision* ahead and astern, and needed the combined efforts of both crews for about 3 hours to complete the job. The photographer was obsessed with repeatedly warning me about a rock that surfaced on my quarter between swells but I told him to disregard it as right alongside it there was 10 fathoms and I always gave a burst ahead in time. Brent Sadler had agreed with me before the operation that the initial figure of £5000 would have to be doubled to £10,000 to cover the risk factor. Lying stopped off Rockall at sunset with a windy, darkening sky, my impression of the disappearing black pinnacle was that it had an evil aura about it - no problem for modern seamen with all their navigational aids but one can only surmise how many were consigned to a watery grave by it and St. Helen's reef in the past.

Above - Rockall with an evil aura
Below - Richard Rose filming the rock

Above - Tom Maclean waving Scottish flag alongside the Automatic
Light. This light was washed away in a winter gale.
Below – transferring equipment for his first night on the ledge.

Donald returning successfully to Scotland with the team –
Sitting on derrick: Donald Patience, Brent Sadler and Mat Anthon
Sitting on shelter deck: Sebastian Rich, David MacLeman and
Richard Rose On main deck: Tom Maclean, his wife Sue, Hamish
Sinclair (mate), Janice Shorten and Tom's pal Rab

Dad's idea of a flat calm day

Recovery of Tom Maclean from Rockall after 40 days.
The sea birds have made use of the shell holes for nesting

Camera man Richard Rose with Tom Maclean being interviewed by Brent Sadler on the ledge

When my son Donald and crew, along with Brent Sadler's and Tom Maclean's crews, 'after forty days', effected the recovery of Tom from the Rock - on a flat calm day - they were able to climb onto it and could see that it was pitted with shell bursts. Apparently it had been used for target practice by U-boats during the war whilst lying in wait for passing convoys.

The pair trawling method of fishing in which I had become involved with Sandy Patience in his boat the *Argosy*, with myself in the *Accumulator*, (re-named *Maureen* in '65), completely revolutionised the catching of pelagic species herring, mackerel and sprats, enabling us to fill up our vessels wherever the shoals appeared. In time we progressed to bigger boats with four times more horsepower than those first two - Sandy now had the *Adventurer* and I the *Vision* and we were able to compete with the modern fleet. On one occasion, when we were fishing for sprats in the South Minch in the seventies - the fishing was very slack by this time - we were told that there was a heavy fishing at the Shields grounds, so we steamed round there. On arrival we found a large fleet of trawlers filling up their vessels, many of which were Danish industrial ones, and one of our fisheries protection cruisers was also in the area. The law at that time was that you could only land sprats if the percentage of herring through the catch was no more than ten per cent. On sampling our first haul among the fleet we found it was more than 50% young herring. We poured it back into the sea, also the next consecutive few tows of often around 60 to 80%. I then said "Sandy, either we fill up our boats, as obviously all the rest of the fleet are doing - it must be that the fisheries cruiser is condoning it - or we have no alternative but to clear out". After the next haul, about 25 tons, I called up the fisheries cruiser and demanded that he board me and sample the first lift as it was clear that all the fleet were catching the same species. He said he was sorry but he had to proceed to another area immediately. I then said "you are only a short distance from me, it will only take you a few minutes", but he cleared off at full speed, obviously embarrassed. We filled our boats, but the situation was that when landing in Shields, or anywhere else in Britain, you could be charged at any time if the fisheries officer happened to check your catch of this mixed haul. It was a crazy situation - you were on tenterhooks all the time the conveyor machine at North Shields was emptying your fishroom. The only market was fish meal. One evening when we were discharging the catch and I was preparing the supper, a man arrived at the galley saying "where's the skipper?" I replied "that's me", and he said "well, you're for the high jump as your catch is over 50% immature herring". I asked "who in the hell are you?" "I'm the assistant fisheries officer", he replied. So I said "forget the monkey, take me to the organ grinder now". Arriving at the office where the head officer was, I was asked what the problem was. I said "put me onto the main fisheries department in London. You know exactly what's going on out there as you're in constant touch with the fisheries cruiser. If there's no high jump for the fleet of industrial trawlers, back off me". He said "calm down, you're all clear this time".

The following week the fishing was to be closed for the Christmas and New Year period so we tied up our boats in a dock beside Swan Hunter's yard, intending to fish there once again when the ports opened. However, as our local fleet were fishing for a similar, but not so mixed, catch at home - mostly less than the 10% - Sandy and I decided to contact Croans, one of the main buyers, and see if he could organise Norwegian klondykers to anchor in the Beauly Firth for us to land to. This was done, and as the Beauly Firth was teeming we both supplied the klondykers the first week, and what I was able to do for the first time was tow the bag alongside them, where they gilsoned the cod end on board one at a time. That week we landed 450 tons with no hassle - a one-off opportunity never again repeated.

On one occasion when I was pair trawling with Sandy in the *Adventurer,* fishing for herring north of the Kyle, he had an engine problem which he expected could be rectified by the engineers in Kyle shipyard, so I had the catch on board the *Vision* to land in Mallaig. Whilst discharging the catch that evening the Harbour Master, a personal friend of mine, informed me that the crew of a Danish ship which had developed a dangerous list which had forced them to abandon ship and then be rescued by the lifeboat, were now in the Marine Hotel. He said "maybe it would be worth your while having a word with them to assess the situation". No further prompting was required for me as every fisherman's dream is the chance of salvage. Not even taking the time to don my Sunday best I met the crew of the *Phoenix* there. They all spoke fluent English and the Captain, John Harkness, told me that they had been hit on the broadside by a heavy sea which shifted the cargo and the vessel had been in imminent danger of capsizing, so they had only had time to drop the anchor with eight shackles of chain and then take to the life raft - fortunately being rescued from that by the Mallaig lifeboat. Weather conditions at the time were force ten. The ship, which had at least a sixty degree list to starboard, had given them no time to recover their personal effects so I borrowed £30 from the manager of the Marine Hotel and we all had a friendly session there. John told me that his cargo consisted of the last shipment of herring from the Isle of Man, salted in plastic barrels, destined for Poland, possibly some of which had been caught by my partner and me. The fact that the amount was only enough to fill the hold three-quarters full had given room for what had happened. He told me that the starboard side was under water almost to the cargo hatch - a few more degrees of list and the ship would go. However he assured me that if there was any possibility of salvage he would contact me but not to hold out much hope and we parted the best of friends.

I rejoined my partner the following day and the next few days consisted of gales and I had completely forgotten to inform Sandy about the possibility of salvage. In fact I expected that the ship had sunk. However, I arrived back in Mallaig on the Friday, having left Sandy once again in the Kyle still troubled with the engine problem, to be told by the Harbour Master, John Murray, that he had been attempting to contact me all week as the *Phoenix* was still afloat and the crew had gone out in a Mallaig boat to attempt to board her but had had to turn back as the weather was too bad and the ship in a dangerous state. Once again meeting the Captain, I suggested contacting Lloyds Underwriters and explained that I was prepared to attempt, in conjunction with my partner vessel, to pair trawl with our combined warps with sixty fathoms of chain connecting our warps from astern of the *Phoenix* up on both sides until the chain in the middle met the anchor, when hopefully we could heave up and break it free and by this method tow the vessel to safety. The insurance agent said they had never heard of such as this but that we had their permission to go ahead. I contacted Sandy and as he expected his repairs to be completed soon he said he would join me the next morning. I had the crew of the *Phoenix* on board as well and fortunately the wind had dropped to flat calm, but the forecast was giving another force ten imminent. However, we arrived alongside the ship and John and his crew boarded, the plan being to jettison the anchor and cable and tow the ship to the nearest pier, which was a small wooden jetty in Talisker, a small loch in Bracadale in Skye, before the next gale.

The ship was listed so far that the chain would not run out but fortunately they had burning gear and were able to cut it free. The lull in the weather placed us in a far more attractive situation. All that was required was that the vessel be towed to safety but the Captain stipulated that he wanted his ship towed with a tow rope from each bow, which I did not think feasible, as one more lurch and the vessel would capsize. So I also had them stream a tow rope with a buoy attached from the quarter of the *Phoenix*. No sooner had we begun to tow from each bow than the ship lurched over to starboard, totally out of control, and John realised that to save it my partner would have to pick up the stern tow rope and go slow astern to hold the vessel stable. This was the way that between us we got the vessel into the sheltered waters by Talisker jetty. The size of the small wooden jetty, only about forty feet long, entailed my partner, tied to one side of the ship, and me on the other side, manoeuvring ahead and astern until eventually it was moored up. The *Phoenix* was about one hundred and eighty feet long and we had to secure ropes on the shore side to hold the vessel fast as the force ten was imminent.

Above - The stricken ship is still afloat against all odds
'throughout a week of severe gales'
Below - Donald rigs up tow rope forward
aboard the Phoenix

Vision shortens up tow rope alongside the ship

Vision starts towing ahead Adventurer astern

Adventurer shortens up the tow-rope astern
Vision behind Phoenix outside Talisker pier
Vision tows the boat to the pier braced alongside

Isle of Man herrings which almost sank a Danish coaster on passage to Poland have turned out to be "Silver Darlings" for the Isle of Skye. At Carbost, where the Phoenix lies with a heavy starboard list, big money is being paid to local "stevedores" unloading most of the 2½ cwt plastic casks to relieve the list.

Last week, in severe storm conditions off the Isle of Rhum, the Phoenix's 7-man crew took to a liferaft when the herring casks shifted and the starboard gunwale became awash. Her Mayday signals were picked up at the Duntulm Coastguard station who quickly called out the Dunvegan coast rescue company and asked all shipping in the area to assist.

In the heavy seas the CalMac "Suilven", on passage to the Clyde for annual overhaul from Stornoway, saw the liferaft light and took the shipwrecked Danes aboard. They were transferred to the Mallaig lifeboat and landed at the mainland port. Last weekend, in unseasonal calm weather, the fishing boats Vision and Adventurer, with Avoch crews, got tow lines aboard the Phoenix as she was held by a single anchor off Talisker Bay in west Skye.

Unmanned, she wallowed between the boats as they towed her to Loch Harport and the safety of the Talisker distillery pier. It has been all hands on deck since then with local labour and machinery handling the slippery casks.

We both agreed that I would stand by the vessel until most of the cargo was shipped ashore with the help of a small mobile crane, so as to get the ship on an even keel and enable them to utilise their own engine to control it when the gale struck. After about twelve hours, when I had made cargo nets from heavy netting which held four barrels at a time, the ship was virtually on an even keel and a field adjacent to the jetty was covered in plastic barrels of herring from the Isle of Man - these supplied the potters in Skye for the next year. The out-of-court settlement, which was a long drawn out process the following year, resulted in my partner and I settling in conjunction for a sum figure of £40,000, which even after legal fees were deducted meant a very profitable day's work.

My partner and I were involved at one time in pair trawling for herring with the *Adventurer* and the *Vision* at the Northumberland coast, landing at Shields, where the herring shoals were prolific, but the time was approaching for us to go to the Isle of Man. Sandy said "what do you think, Donald? We are doing okay - shall we stay or go to the Isle of Man?" I said "Sandy, have gas, will travel; let's go". We fuelled up, went round the top through the Pentland Firth and down to the Isle of Man. Two days later, approaching the area, Sandy said "we have left a good fishing at Shields but the reports today are very poor, only eight units were caught last night at the Douglas grounds". I said "Sandy, this is the right time to arrive there - if every boat was full up we would be too late". Sandy said "Donald, you are an optimist, I am a pessimist". This was when approaching the Calf of Man Sound and we saw the Fisheries cruiser steaming slowly south of Peel. No sooner had we cleared the Sound than I saw a sea-angling boat off Port Saint Mary catching fish about one mile offshore. The sonar showed a massive shoal of herring right underneath the boat, obviously the cod were feeding off it, so I shot the trawl astern of the angling boat and told Sandy to swallow that boat. This, as Sandy also could see with his sonar, was where the shoal was. It was midday; we towed with one hundred and fifty fathoms of warp and after twenty minutes the bag leapt to the surface with over three hundred units of herring which we towed outside the three mile limit and landed in Port Saint Mary. This was the start of another successful Isle of Man fishing.

In my 50 years as a fisherman I had been skipper of 4 vessels but will never forget the winter when we fished the Kessock herring in the skaffie the *Pathfinder* which we had on hire from the local hotelier at the time when the *Guiding Star* was being built. When one considers today's state-of-the-art technology - fishfinders, sonar, net monitors and other gadgets which are all taken for granted on today's modern fishing boats and with ever-depleting fish stocks are essential to make them viable - only reverting to sail could have been more basic than fishing with the skaffie. A 13-15hp Kelvin engine, a tiny basic stove, and everyone's *kistick* – the latter a rectangular box to hold your week's provisions with a lift-off lid which you rested on your knees to serve as a tray. The *kistick* was about 2 feet long and 1 foot deep and wide, with a rope strap spliced at either end to enable you to sling it on your shoulder. These were made by the local carpenter and undertaker, Donald Scorock, possibly from off-cuts whilst making coffins, and when I bought my first one the price was 5 shillings (25p). Collecting your first *kistick* was the initial step to becoming a full-time fisherman and would be equivalent to today's successful yuppie owning his first Porsche. As this was before the echo sounder had come into vogue you were then completely dependent on *appearance* - sometimes the shoals were so prolific you could even smell them, which was expressed as a 'green air'. The first shot at the close, however, you always shot the full fleet, especially in the Beauly Firth where the main area at the close was known as the South

Trough and stretched from the sea lock of the Caledonian Canal to Redcastle point. This trink was where the herring congregated at the first of the flood before moving up the Beauly Firth as the tide came in. Quite often the first boats to shoot would witness the buoys going under as soon as the nets hit the water and on many occasions no sooner were they shot than you could haul back with your quota, which was set per man according to the market's requirements. Another essential to have on board was a long slender pole from 15 to 18 feet long for sounding the water, called a *boamie,* which enabled you to navigate the narrow channels between the sandbanks in the Beauly Firth. Also, quite often you could feel the herring striking against it in these dense shallow waters. Most of the boats had a hand aldis lamp in the stem of the boat to see the herring swimming in the water but on the *Pathfinder* we made do with a bicycle torch which did the job okay. As the shoals moved up with the flood tide and back down on the ebb the small shallow-draughted skaffies had the advantage over the bigger boats, especially in the Beauly Firth when, with the flood tide, the further up you could go the more herring you caught - hence the expression "they are right up in the neeps (turnips)". With everyone trying to go as far up as possible and haul back before too much ebb, then navigate down the winding channels to the deep water from the sea lock across to Charleston, it was inevitable that occasionally when hauling a heavy catch some boat or boats became stranded.

One particularly exceptional cold spell we were hauling on the ebb, well up the Firth, when sheets of ice floating down and sliding against the canvas buoys cut them, so that the nets which were heavily fished were now virtually anchored and the boat grounded on the Redcastle bank. However, we were able to drag the remaining nets on board with about 30 crans of herring, which was about the capacity for the *Pathfinder* - no option now but for all hands to turn in, close the hatch and await the next flood. At daylight, which was about low water, when my father lifted the hatch he called out "stay in your beds; don't move as we are balanced on an even keel right on the edge of the bank with a steep drop on the starboard side". He slid the hatch back on and then said "well boys I've never seen this before, the boat is on a point of balance - if she lists off we are done for, don't even fart". Thankfully we floated off okay about 3pm and steaming back down we encountered the first of the fleet on their way up. This was the *Forager* and the skipper Sandy hailed us and shouted, "Where are you making for?" To which my father replied "Ijmuiden". This at that time was the top herring port in Holland - his sense of humour never failed him.

It is hard to convey to someone who hasn't experienced it how at one with nature and contented life could be on board a skaffie, let alone have him believe how men found it possible to live, dine and sleep in such a confined space. Your only light was a 6-watt bulb (at least we had electricity) and the heat and glow of the bogie stove. Combine this with the smell of cooking, and my Uncle Will's pipe of black twist with the fags which my father smoked incessantly, and you can imagine what the atmosphere was like - forget passive smoking! One of the main ingredients in everyone's k*istick* was a large dome of skaff (mashed potatoes) prepared before leaving home on a plate and sliced up and fried up along with most meals. Cooking facilities consisted of one large frying pan, shared by all, where everything from Kessock herring, skaff and whatever else, to occasionally, top-of-the-range steak was blended in and supplemented with a large enamel teapot. Your k*istick* and a ten-gallon portable water tank were topped up daily on landing and everyone thrived on this basic way of life. Sleeping facilities consisted of the chaff sack, the chaff obtained from the local farm at threshing time. I often reflect on those days and wonder if it is not possible that in this modern age, with all the hype we are constantly being brainwashed by, we have lost most of our natural immunity regarding food. If we were to absorb all the fresh dangers we are constantly being warned of, we could well end up in a sterile world where virtually nothing was safe to eat.

The local hotelier, Mr Howie, who owned the *Pathfinder,* was delighted to have his boat fishing and told my father that if there was anything he required for the boat just to order it. So as the *Guiding Star* was being built at the time my father purchased a canvas fishroom hatch-cover 24 feet by 18 feet which, when one considered that the hatch on the *Pathfinder* was about 6 feet by 8 feet, was slightly excessive but was never queried.

Later that winter when fishing the Invergordon Firth and had only a few crans of herring, not enough to steam to Inverness, my father decided to tie up for the day at Invergordon pier. He had served as a minesweeper skipper during the war and as his fishing boat the *Ormond Hill* had been run down by an Aberdeen liner in 1944 he had decided to remain in the navy for a further year after the war. He obtained the position of captain of a tank landing craft based at Invergordon. This TLC was fitted out with a sophisticated long range camera that followed the trajectory of a shell from the time of its being fired from the destroyer's gun at the firing range at Golspie to its landing in the sea. This was to determine the loss in fall of shot caused by wear in the rifling. He had been told that the camera cost over £15,000 and this exercise entailed his being moored alongside the particular destroyer involved.

No sooner were we tied up at Invergordon pier than he told us that he had been a great pal of the commander of the naval base at that time and he went up to see if the same man was still in charge. Arriving back a short time later he told us we were to go up to the naval stores as his pal had said "the war's over now Donald, and as you're building a new boat, if there's anything suitable, help yourself". This was in 1947. It was an opportunity not to be missed and we started with a few coils of rope, then as space was limited on the skaffie, a galvansied 3/8" 50-fathom chain closed the deal - with the base well supplied with Kessock herring. The coils of rope and the chain were driven down to the boat courtesy of the naval truck - this was at about low water and when paying down the end of the chain it took charge and crashed down on the deck and caused it to collapse, but the base had an ample supply of timber and a naval carpenter who was able to shore it back into shape for us.

My father had the TLC from 1945 to 1946 and we had a few trips on it as it was off-duty most weekends. One weekend he brought it round to Avoch, where a crowd of us rowed out in a skiff and were all given a trip. It was powered with two 500hp Paxman Ricardo engines and at full speed was capable of 18 knots in calm water, so we had a good day out courtesy of the Royal Navy. One day when he had to shelter from a gale which had caused suspension of operations at the firing range, he dropped anchor inside the Dornoch Firth at Meikle Ferry. On heaving up it was discovered that the anchor had become fast on the telephone cable and subsequently parted it, but the fact that the cable had not been marked on his Admiralty chart meant he could not be held responsible. However, when he was told it was the main line to the north of Scotland and that the break was causing major disruption, also that their cable-laying vessel was down in London, he said "get a replacement cable, I'll soon lay it for you", as the TLC was ideally suited to this operation. The following day a new telephone cable arrived, was taken on board and he had it laid in under half an hour - whereas the original one had apparently taken six weeks to lay.

My final trip at sea was to Rockall and began as usual. Before leaving I contacted Benbecula weather station to get the long range forecast for the next few days, which is generally spot on. Verdict, no more than force 6. We arrived at the Rockall grounds on the Monday night with about a force 6, shot the trawl and after four hours heaved up for twelve boxes – a poor haul. It was now blowing a full gale. I called up the fisheries cruiser who was patrolling this area, the *Sulskier,* to get his long range forecast. He said at least gale force for the next few days no indication of it moderating, so I decided to clear out and make for the Sound of Harris and fish the Minch waters. The wind was NW with a heavy sea running so we set the watch for the Sound. Approaching the sound the following morning the *Vision* was very sluggish in the water, but with the heavy sea running it was only when we were in the calm water of the Minch that you could see that the boat was away down by the head, and when lifting the fishroom hatch we saw that the hold was nearly full of water with smashed fish boxes and the remains of 12 tons of ice wallowing about. I immediately told the crew to put on their life jackets and man the deck bilge pumps. I turned back inshore, contacted the Stornoway coastguard explaining the situation and after about half an hour we could see that the water level was going down. The only problem was that with all the debris the pumps were often choking.

I got in touch with the harbourmaster in Loch Maddy, asked him to have the fire engine ready on the pier for our arrival which he did. With the aid of the fire engine pump and willing helpers, the fishroom was pumped dry and the remnants of 450 smashed fish boxes cleared away. My son Donald put on his diving gear and went over the side to check the hull. What I had first suspected was that the sonar dome had been ripped off but this was not so and after about twenty minutes he came back on board having found no damage, though as he said "the water is not very clear". What we next thought was that the fishroom bilge pump had been suctioned back from the sea which can happen if the valve is not sitting properly, so I decided to set off for Stornoway as most of the fishroom insulation had been ripped off by the 12 tons of ice wallowing around the hold. However, we were only under way for a short time when my son said "the water is over the fishroom floor again" which required the pump once more. So the slip in Stornoway was the only answer. Arriving there we were told to ebb the *Vision* on cement blocks at no 2 jetty where we saw a perforated spot which collapsed when tapped with a hammer. When the boat was slipped and they were lifting the fishroom floor, which was caulked and bolted, they found a strip of the hull between the sonar dome and a transducer pitted like cheese. The verdict was electrosis but a complete sonic survey of the rest of the hull found no more affected areas. When the surveyor inspected the hold he estimated that there had been about 150 tons of water when we first opened the hatch - for the crew and the *Vision* it had been a close thing, once again luck was on our side. It was shortly afterwards that I had the two hip replacements and as the knee kept flaring up as well and my general health condition was poor, I was strongly advised to end my career at sea.

Like most Avoch fishermen I acquired a nickname (byname) - in my case, "Flake" - from the fact that whereas other skippers would tell their crews to" lay" on the nets or trawl or repair them, I got into the habit of saying "flake" them on. I only became aware of my title when, after wrecking the *Guiding Star* and being berthed on the *Aspire*, I said to one of the crew "what or who is this Flake you keep referring to?". As Donald was by far the commonest name in the village - and even on the *Aspire* there were three of us - I had become labelled for life.

Index of Photos

Page 50	Guiding Star at prawns in Moray Firth - school holidays 1967 Crew left to right - William Patience; Roddy Reid; Frankie Kemp; Arthur Macarthur and myself in front. In wheelhouse skipper Donald Patience
Pages 53/6	Sketches by Davy MacLeman artist, poet & retired marine engineer
Page 82	Scarborough Evening News - Donald Patience and Donald Macleod mending nets on Scarborough North Wharf
Page 91	Avoch herring fleet – Whitby 1969 Skipper of 'Heather Lea' Andrew W Macleman in front
Page 92	Avoch herring fleet – Scarborough 1969 Avoch fishing fleet - Scarborough 1969
Page 104	The Kimara FR178, Skipper Charles Duthie, ashore in Loch Broom, Ullapool Loch after hurricane of 1982 - all boats refloated successfully. (dad's advice to me always have a 'rope ashore' - never leave your boat at anchor)
Page 105	Guiding Star in her safe berth - Ullapool harbour
Page 110	The 'Wreck of the Guiding Star' - James Jack
Page 113	Maureen INS 215 leaving Avoch Harbour 1968 - courtesy Donald Macleman
Page 120	Dad and myself during summer holidays in the cabin of the Maureen in Bunsen Harbour, Isle of Mull
Page 121	Dad and myself working the winch – prawn fishing 1971 aboard the Maureen (not the same Health & Safety Rules in 'them days')
Page 138	Adventurer INS 8 - Skipper Sandy Patience A poor day off Barra Head - 1980
Page 146	The Vision OB 390 - Mallaig 1975
Page 147	The Vision before re-registered OB 390
Page 151	Above - Rockall with an evil aura Below - Richard Rose filming the rock
Page 152	Above - Tom Maclean waving Scottish flag alongside the Automatic Light. This light was washed away in a winter gale. Below – transferring equipment for his first night on the ledge.
Page 153	Donald returning successfully to Scotland with the team – Sitting on derrick: Donald Patience, Brent Sadler and Mat Anthon Sitting on shelter deck: Sebastian Rich, David MacLeman and Richard Rose On main deck: Tom Maclean, his wife Sue, Hamish Sinclair (mate), Janice Shorten and Tom's pal Rab

Acknowledgements

Special thanks are due to Fortrose Medical Centre,
Dr Alexander MacGregor, Dr Will Fraser and Raigmore
Hospital

Frankie Macleman - typing original manuscript

William Ramsay McGhee - computer work

Catherin Deveney and Margaret Mackenzie – proof reading

Avoch Fishermans Co-op and dad's pals for photos

Gael Force Marine Ltd, Inverness - Stewart Graham and Ben
Davidson

His old friend Ewen France in Stornoway

Rev Richard Burkitt and Kevin Swanson at For The Right
Reasons

David MacLeman - for sketches

The poem "The Wreck of the Guiding Star" - James Jack

APPENDICES

1. Recollections from Donnie Macleod - Ullapool

During the 1960's Ullapool was still a major herring port, playing host to the many herring drifters during their annual migration following the shoals around the country.

It was at this time I was appointed ^Mv Master, having served my engineering apprenticeship at John Brown, Clydebank and spent a few interesting years on deep sea ships.

Ullapool, at that time, did not have plentiful berthing space and there was always a squachle for the drifters to get their samples up to the sale ring and their catches landed to the pier. The sale times were dictated by the Government Fisheries Dept, which only permitted sales on weekdays. This consequently led to the boats lying idle at the weekends when they would either anchor in the bay or seek a berth alongside the pier.

The skippers were all doughty fishermen, and none more so than one, Donald Patience from Avoch.

Donald came in to the Harbour office one day, and after pleasant chatty introductions to one another, before departing he presented me with a post card showing the f.v. Accumulator tied up alongside the inner side of the pier.

"There, Donnie", he said, "that's where my boat is usually tied up on Friday nights", and so, my first encounter with this remarkable man.

Over the subsequent herring seasons Donald showed amazing inventiveness in trying to secure this prized berth for a weekend tie up. VHF radio was just coming in to play, but in Ullapool, with the surrounding hills, the range was very limited. One of his VHF calls to the Harbour office was to tell me that he needed a berth as his bow thruster had packed in. Bow thruster??? - on a wooden fishing boat!!! They didn't even have them on passenger liners in those days. Another wheeze was to call in and say his variable pitch propeller was jammed and he was being towed in by his partner, Sandy, and needed a berth alongside - variable pitch had only just been invented.

The VHP radio was of course open for all to hear - no private channels in those days - and it wasn't long until the other skippers cottoned on to this. Just about every boat in the fleet suddenly had "bow thrusters", "auto pilots" etc, so I had to revert to allocating that berth only to the desperately needy, and try to sort out some of the fanciful claims, not always successfully.

Donald was one of those skippers who always kept a cautious eye on the various pronouncements coming out of the Scottish Office Fisheries Dept, and was never slow to respond by telephoning from his agent's office to forcibly make his comments known. On one occasion the fishery cruiser was scheduled to berth after the evening ferry to

Stornoway had departed. Donald somehow found out that the Fisheries Minister was on board. He appeared in my office to tell me he was going to meet the Minister (uninvited, of course) when the ship docked, but "Where can I get a haircut" he said. At this time of day all the barbers were shut. I then remembered that the chandlers wife (Patricia) had been a hairdresser, so I sent Donald up, and he duly got his hair cut in the back store of the grocer's shop. Back to the office he came, hair neat and tidy, but his jacket was torn a wee bit here and there. "Donnie, have you got a jacket I could wear" he said, " Naw, you're no the right size". I noticed the corner shop across the road had a rail of jackets on display outside, so I suggested he make enquiries of the owner to borrow a jacket temporarily. Back he came suitably attired and I noticed his own torn jacket neatly hanging on the clothes rail with the others.

The fisheries vessel duly berthed, and as soon as the gangway touched the pier, Donald was up there like a shot. How he got on with the Minister, I never found out, as he was off back to sea that evening.

About an hour later however, I noticed the torn jacket was gone, and his moment of finery was back on the display rail outside the shop. Whether he ever asked the proprietor or not, was never mentioned.

There were many other meetings which were often humourous and warm. My memory of Donald is of a genuine gentle man who never aspired to being wealthy, he was too generous to others - a giving man, only wishing a best price for his catch to help his crew. I always considered Donald more of a friend than a visiting skipper. Sadly missed by all who knew him.

2. Carnegie Hero Fund Trustees Award to Donald Patience

"Donald Patience (13), Schoolboy, 11 James Street, Avoch, Ross-shire, on 16th July 1914, rescued another boy from drowning at Avoch Harbour.

About 4.30pm on 16th July 1914, a boy (11), while bathing at the Harbour, Avoch, got beyond his depth in 6 feet of water, and, being unable to swim, was in danger of drowning.

Donald Patience, who, with other boys, was in the vicinity at the time, and observed the boy struggling in the water, immediately, without removing any of his clothing, dived in to his assistance. With some difficulty, Patience got one hand under the boy's chin and the other under his arms, and, by using his feet, he was able to swim with the boy to the shallow water, a distance of about 12 yards. Both boys were then able to walk ashore".

The Carnegie Hero Fund Trustees awarded a silver watch with an inscription to Donald Patience.

The Carnegie Hero Fund Trustees awarded a silver watch with an inscription to Donald Patience

THE CARNEGIE DUNFERMLINE
AND HERO FUND TRUSTEES

Annual Report & Accounts 2008

CARNEGIE
HERO FUND TRUST

14 July 2009

Donald Patience
6 Deans Road
Fortrose
Ross-shire
IV10 8TJ

Dear Mr Patience,

Thank you for your letter requesting information about the incident that led to your grandfather's heroism being recognised by the Carnegie Hero Fund Trust and I now enclose some details.

In addition to the award of an inscribed silver pocket watch, Donald Patience's name was entered in the Roll of Honour, a beautifully illustrated book that is kept on permanent display in the Andrew Carnegie Birthplace Museum here in Dunfermline. It contains the names of over 6,000 people whose heroism has been recognised by the Trustees since the foundation of the Hero Fund Trust in 1908.

I enclose a pamphlet giving details of the Museum along with a copy of our most recent annual report and a photograph of the page from the Roll of Honour relating to your grandfather's heroism.

The Museum recently re-opened after undergoing a major upgrade and is proving very popular with visitors. If you are ever in the area, I am sure you would enjoy a visit to see the Roll of Honour for yourself. Please give us a ring in advance and we shall arrange to have the Roll opened at the relevant page.

With kind regards,

Hele MacDonald

Nora T C Rundell

ANDREW CARNEGIE HOUSE, PITTENCRIEFF STREET
DUNFERMLINE, FIFE KY12 8AW
TEL: 01383 723638 FAX: 01383 749799 E-MAIL: herofund@carnegietrust.com
CHIEF EXECUTIVE: NORA T C RUNDELL BA MBA MCMI REGISTERED CHARITY NO. SCO 00729

182

GEORGE A. COOMES.
(29), North Kensington, on the 10th
July, 1914, rescued a boy (5½) from drowning in the Grand Junction Canal at North
Kensington.

JAMES MASSIE. (16),
ABERDEEN, on the 9th July, 1914,
endeavoured to rescue, and on the
same occasion

OLAFUR ARNASON.
(54), ABERDEEN, succeeded in rescuing
a boy from drowning in the River Dee.—

JOHN FRYER. (20),
Newcastle-on-Tyne, on the 3rd July,
1914, was instrumental in rescuing
from drowning in the River Tyne a man
who was attempting to commit suicide.

THOMAS WALSH.
(25), WATERFORD, on the 5th July, 1914,
rescued a boy from drowning in the River Suir
at Waterford Brickworks.

DONALD PATIENCE.
(13), AVOCH, on the 16th July, 1914, rescued a boy (11) from drowning at Avoch Harbour.

3. Dad's last letter to Fishing News

As I reflect on my childhood days and the post war years right up to the seventies when Edward Heath initially handed overall our fishing rights to the E.E.C. we had some of the richest fishing grounds in the world.

Sadly exasperated by following governments to approaching a stage when white fish fishermen in Britain could become history.

This Nation is unique in that it is the only island nation worldwide that regards its fishermen as being expendable otherwise it would have retained the 200 mile limit.

One does not require to be a Marine Biologist to understand this.

I have in my lifetime as a fisherman witnessed the decimation of the stocks since our fishing grounds became a free for all rather than a National Heritage to be protected at all costs for future generations of fishermen.

One prime example of how our fishermen are discriminated against is three years ago when the West Coast deep water stocks were being allocated by the Powers that be. Scotland fishermen were granted 2% while France and Spain were given the remaining 98% thereby rendering the most modern Scottish white fish vessels obsolete with no quota.

4. Decommissioning of Scottish Fishing Boats

Dad's view on the wanton destruction of fishing boats to comply with Government Rules.

Scrapping boats carried out at the Thornbush Slip - this was a criminal waste of resources.

Boats could have been sold out of the country, used in the leisure industry as houseboats, whale/dolphin watch, leisure or dive support.

It ripped the soul out of the fishermen who had spent their lives on these vessels which had been their home and carried them safely through some of the worst seas in the world. What hope was there for the Industry if they would do this to their boats?

5. Tribute to Hamish Sinclair

Thanks to Hamish who acted as Logistics Co-ordinator during the training program conducted on the dark waters of Loch Ness in the shadow of Urquhart Castle.

To Subsea Services who supplied the fast rescue boat.

To Ken Hooper and Mat Anthon for safely supervising the climbing, absailing and transferring from the Vision to the small boats and onto the cliffs around that forbidding fortress.

For returning to Rockall to take Tom Maclean back to Scotland after 40 days on the Rock. This let my father take a much needed holiday with my mother in his beloved Portugal. Sadly returning, with mounting health problems, on his last summer at sea.

6. Thanks to Sandy and Ian Patience

Thanks to Sandy and Ian Patience for supplying the transport to move my father's old nylon nets to Fraserburgh where William Whyte ('Forever Grateful' FR 249) processed and sold the scrap nylon.

The Bethel Fellowship Trust used some of the proceeds to build boats for fishermen after the Indonesian Tsunami in Burma.

Praise the Lord

Rev. David Prakasam
Bethel Fellowship Trust
Coimbatore

Dear Pastor,

Through Pastor David Prakasam, Bethel Fellowship
Trust, Coimbatore, In the month of July I received
a fiber boat and engine net and other fishing
materials.. We thank the sponsors.

With the help of this boat and net we go fishing everyday. We were in lot of trouble and
were struggling when tsunami tragedy struck on our families. But with this boat, engine
and fishing nets we every day go into the sea for fishing. Every day we are able to get
variety of fishes, shrimps, prawns, crabs, etc. by trading all this we are happy.

We once again thank and convey our good wishes to Dr. David Prakasam, Rev. T. Jacob
Manoharan, sponsors and benefactors.

Signed

Kirubai
Anjappan
Elamairajan
Sivaraj
Nithya

Praise the Lord
Sender
D Antony Raj
Aanya Nattu Theru
Nagappatinam

Through
Respected Director
Bethel Fellowship Trust
Coimbatore

Sub thanks letter

Sir

I thank you for the nets and boat which you had given two months ago   I and
my sons are catching fishing and continuing our trade I shall never forget your
favour throughout my life   I and my family are praying for you everyday and
request you to pray for me and my family

Yours truly
Antony Raj
Nagapattinam
15 11 07

192

7. Obituary Donald Patience
1931-2007
Leading Skipper and Personality
Fishing News 14/Sept/2007

Donald Patience well known Scottish skipper and fishing industry personality, died on the 16th of July after several years of ill-health.

He was born in Avoch on 1 January 1931 into a Family with a long association with the fishing. When he left school he started working in the forestry and then got a berth on a local boat the Boy Jim.

At 18 he was called up to do his two years National Service in the Royal Navy and on completion of this he went back fishing - this time onboard the Guiding Star, a new boat for his father, his brother George and himself. Donald went on to skipper this boat.

While onboard the Guiding Star, which like many of the boats from the North East fished the autumn during the herring spawning season at Whitby, Donald met and married Maureen, who was nursing in Whitby at the time.
Donald and Maureen would have celebrated their Golden Wedding next Month.

At Whitby too, Donald won five trophies for his fishing effort. He passed his ticket in 1958 in what must have been a record time - four weeks. Maureen remembers him travelling home on the back of a motorbike to Avoch! Donald was also skipper of the Accumulator, Maureen and Vision - 20 years neighbouring ourselves for herring mackerel and sprats, indeed he worked at the lines, the drifts, the ring net, the trawl, white fish, gillnets and prawns.

Donald was one of life's richest tapestries. His presence, personality, great wit and pioneering spirit, along with his kind manner, endeared him to all who met and worked with him. He could be a politician as all those in office who crossed his path paid attention to what he had to write and say.

One of the highlights of Donald's career was when he negotiated the salvage of the Phoenix, which had run into difficulties and cargo had shifted off Skye. The Phoenix ironically, was one of the lugers that took our herring at the Isle of Man.

Donald entertained the Lloyds representative to the best of highland hospitality when this successful effort was completed.

Donald was always willing to help others - whether it was at sea or in the village where he spent his entire life.

He will be sorely missed by his family and friends. Our sympathy is extended to Maureen his son Donald and his daughters Jacqueline and Alison and his grand children.

We feel sure that readers of FN will also miss his interesting letters. AJP

8.Tribute to Royal National Mission to Deep Sea Fishermen

Thanks to Superintendant William Simmonds and all the staff of the Missions around the country who helped us and the crew of our boat.

Wreck of boat outside the Mission in Lochinver in 1987.
The Mission is now closed.

9. Tribute to Denholm Fishselling Ltd Trading as George Walker and Sons

Thanks to Jimmy, Colin and all the staff in the offices around Scotland.

This was the Vision 0B 390 in 1981 conducting a Government Survey of cod stocks in Northern Scottish waters. Dad was passionate about conserving fish stocks and passive fishing which is now carried out by many inshore boats in the fleet.

Gill Netting, Save Fuel, Save Cod Stocks, Save Fisherman.

10. Donald's Retirement
By Maureen Patience

Donald's retirement started at the age of 57.

Being free from pain after two successful hip replacement operations and never one for 'golf or the garden', he felt he had to occupy himself so he started to repair and make nets and cover prawn creels.

Although he had a purpose built net store, my kitchen was taken over with his requests for various nets as he said it gave his hands physiotherapy and his brain stimulation. As he was unable to stand for long periods, he made equipment to extend the kitchen table to enable him to sit while working.

He was content sitting working at his nets or writing 'his book' or listening to music on the radio. The grandchildren were familiar seeing grandad in the kitchen and sometimes helping him with his work. Donald would watch the programs on politics and if he did not agree with anything said he would have to write in to 'state his opinion'.

The highlight of his week was reading the Fishing News but once again if something bugged him out would come the pen, 'to stand up for fishermen'.

He loved to go on holiday to the Algarve in Portugal, watching from the balcony of our hotel the small boats fishing for sardines at night and the next morning going into Portamo and enjoying the sardines cooked on the brazier.

It reminded him of the sights and smells of days long ago, when the 'kessocks' were cooked in Avoch.

In 2000, Donald suffered a heart attack but with prompt attention from Dr Macgregor and the staff in Raigmore Hospital and a strict warning to stop smoking and lead a quiet life, he was home in a month. Unfortunately his rheumatoid arthritis had progressed, so writing became an effort.

Donald had to overcome more than the average share of personal tragedies 'too hard to mention' but we are left with such happy memories.

If this book helps to save one life it has been worth all the time and effort put in by Donald and all concerned.

11. Tribute to Highland Libraries

Thanks to all the staff in the Highland Libraries.

Dad loved books: reading was one of his greatest pleasures. As his illness progressed his mobility became greatly impaired. As a primary carer with the only car, we used Inverness Library as a pickup point as they have first class disabled facilities and a friendly caring staff.
He would love to have known that there is a copy of his memories in the British Library.

12. Bens E'mail From Gael Force

"I was privileged enough to know Donald Patience for around 15 years since I joined Gael Force Marine. I always enjoyed the craic with Donald when I delivered his nets & mending twine & we would chew the fat about the state of the fishing industry & his own times at sea. On leaving he would give me a wink & say "Wait there a minute Ben" he'd disappear & return after a couple of minutes with a bag of the famous Donald Patience fish cakes, which were enjoyed by all the Davidson family. On leaving I would shout back "You'll need to give me the recipe for them sometime" to which he would always reply with a wink & a big grin, "I cannae tell ye that boy". His sense of humour & wit were second to none.

A true grafter & a gentleman, an inspiration to anyone who made his acquaintance.

It's not much Donald but it's something that always comes back to me when someone mentions your fathers name.

Say hello to your mam for me & I hope she is keeping well.

Best regards

Ben Davidson Purchasing Manager Gael Force Marine Ltd."